INDIA SINCE 1980

This book considers the remarkable transformations that have taken place in India since 1980, a period that began with the assassination of the formidable Prime Minister Indira Gandhi. Her death, and that of her son Rajiv seven years later, marked the end of the Nehru-Gandhi era. Although the country remains one of the few democracies in the developing world, many of the policies instigated by these earlier regimes have been swept away to make room for dramatic alterations in the political, economic, and social landscape. Sumit Ganguly and Rahul Mukherji, two leading political scientists of South Asia, chart these developments with particular reference to social and political mobilization, the rise of the Bharatiya Janata Party and its challenge to Nehruvian secularism, and the changes to foreign policy that, in combination with its meteoric economic development, have ensured India a significant place on the world stage. The book is intended for students and anyone interested in understanding this diverse, energetic, and youthful democracy.

Sumit Ganguly is Professor of Political Science and the Rabindranath Tagore Chair in Indian Cultures and Civilizations at Indiana University, Bloomington. He is the author of numerous books, including *India's Foreign Policy: Retrospect and Prospect* (2010); *Nuclear Proliferation in South Asia* (2008), with S. Paul Kapur; and *The Routledge Handbook of Asian Security Studies* (2010), coedited with Andrew Scobell and Joseph Liow. He is currently at work on a new book, *Deadly Impasse: Indo-Pakistani Relations at the Dawn of a New Century*.

Rahul Mukherji is Associate Professor of South Asian Studies at the National University of Singapore. He is the editor of *India's Economic Transition: The Politics of Reforms* (2007) and *India: The Political Economy of Reforms* (2004), coedited with Bibek Debroy.

THE WORLD SINCE 1980

This new series is designed to examine politics, economics, and social change in important countries and regions during the past three decades. No prior background knowledge of a given country will be required by readers. The books are written by leading social scientists.

Volumes published

Brazil Since 1980; Francisco Vidal Luna and Herbert S. Klein

Europe Since 1980; Ivan T. Berend

Israel Since 1980; Guy Ben-Porat, Yagil Levy, Shlomo Mizrahi, Ayre Naor, and Erez Tzfadia

Japan Since 1980; Thomas F. Cargill and Takayuki Sakamoto

Mexico Since 1980; Stephen Haber, Herbert S. Klein, Noel Maurer, and Kevin J. Middlebrook

Russia Since 1980; Steven Rosefielde and Stefan Hedlund

The United States Since 1980; Dean Baker

Volumes in preparation

China Since 1980; Ross Garnaut

France Since 1980; Timothy Smith

Iran Since 1980; Ali Ansari

Turkey Since 1980; Sevket Pamuk and Yesim Arat

INDIA SINCE 1980

Sumit Ganguly

Indiana University, Bloomington

Rahul Mukherji

National University of Singapore

CAMBRIDGE UNIVERSITY PRESS
Cambridge, New York, Melbourne, Madrid, Cape Town,
Singapore, São Paulo, Delhi, Tokyo, Mexico City

Cambridge University Press
32 Avenue of the Americas, New York, NY 10013-2473, USA

www.cambridge.org
Information on this title: www.cambridge.org/9780521678049

First published 2011

Printed in the United States of America

A catalog record for this publication is available from the British Library.

Library of Congress Cataloging in Publication Data
Ganguly, Sumit.
  India Since 1980 / Sumit Ganguly, Rahul Mukherji.
     p.   cm. – (The world since 1980)
  Includes bibliographical references and index.
  ISBN 978-0-521-86093-2 (hardback) – ISBN 978-0-521-67804-9 (paperback)
  1. India – History – 1947–   2. India – Social conditions – 1947–
  3. India – Economic conditions – 1947–   4. India – Politics and
  government – 1977–   I. Mukherji, Rahul, 1967–   II. Title.
  DS480.853.G374   2011
  954.05–dc22   2010045940

ISBN 978-0-521-86093-2 Hardback
ISBN 978-0-521-67804-9 Paperback

Sumit Ganguly dedicates this book to the memory of Professor William John Schafer of Berea College.

Rahul Mukherji dedicates this book to his father Professor Partha Nath Mukherji.

research assistant. I owe a great deal to the students at the National University of Singapore who attended my classes on Indian politics and political economy. The chapter titled "India's Economic Transformation" benefited from an invited lecture at the Australian National University. My family – Anjali, Ayon, and Adheesh – made this project theirs as well. I was supported in this book project by an Academic Research Fund Tier 1 grant from the Faculty of Arts and Social Sciences of the National University of Singapore. – Rahul Mukherji

1

Four Revolutions and India's Future

For the better part of the past three decades the Indian polity has been in the throes of four revolutionary changes. They are in the realms of political mobilization, secularism, foreign policy, and economic policy making. These transformations have not moved in tandem but have overlapped with one another. Nevertheless, they collectively represent a steady and potentially fundamental remaking of many features of the Indian political landscape.

Of the four transformative movements, the social revolution in India has been in the making for perhaps the longest time span. It involves the rise of India's lower castes especially in northern India, from what Marx once referred to in another, but related, context as "the sleep of ages." Such a revolutionary upsurge had already taken place in southern India during the 1960s. Now through the process of growing media exposure, increased literacy, and, above all, through participation in local, regional, and national elections, India's hitherto dispossessed are finding their political voice. Since the 1980s this process has accelerated and altered the texture of Indian politics dramatically by throwing into disarray long-held assumptions about the predictable voting behavior of the lower castes. Instead of routinely turning to the once-dominant Congress Party, lower-caste voters have demonstrated much-greater independence and have switched their loyalties to local, ethnic, and regional parties. Accordingly, their political unpredictability has made and unmade governments at state and national levels. There is little reason to believe that this growing political sophistication will come to a close in the foreseeable future. Instead, the dramatic process of political mobilization under way promises to steadily erode upper-caste dominance in Indian politics and to make India a more representative polity.

The rising political consciousness and acumen of lower castes along with occasional political alliances with north India's Muslim communities has posed a threat not only to the dominance of the Congress Party but also to an upper-caste-based political order. This challenge, along with other contingent developments in Indian politics, generated a backlash against India's secular order from the mid-1980s. The Hindu chauvinist Bharatiya Janata Party (BJP) rode the crest of high-caste anxieties and sought to adumbrate them in the political arena. Thanks to its deft exploitation of upper-caste misgivings, throughout the 1990s its political rise appeared inexorable and the fate of Indian secularism appeared rather dire. However, the seeming willingness of the BJP and a number of its ancillary organizations, including the Rashtriya Swayamsevak Sangh (RSS) and the Vishwa Hindu Parishad (VHP), to create permissive conditions for much political violence directed against minorities may have contributed to the decline of its initial appeal. That said, the BJP through the relentless pursuit of its antisecular agenda when in and out of office during the 1990s and beyond managed to change the terms of political discourse in India. The taboo in Indian politics against the explicit scapegoating of minorities suffered under the BJP's assiduous antisecular barrage. Though it suffered significant defeats in two national elections (2004 and 2009) it would be premature to write off the BJP as a spent force in Indian politics. An antisecular strain has long existed in Indian politics and was present in substantial measure during India's anticolonial nationalist struggle. Consequently, this strand of India's political culture can again be drawn upon under particular circumstances if dexterously resurrected.

Although Indian secularism is not moribund or faced with an imminent demise, it does face potentially formidable challenges in the future. If the BJP and its associates were able to undermine the secular order, India would cease to be a liberal democracy as it would effectively consign its religious minority to the status of second-class citizens. The long-term survival of Indian secularism is critical to the health of India's democratic polity.

Since the early 1980s, India's policy makers have also chosen to challenge another cornerstone of the Indian polity, namely the commitment to a strategy of state-led economic growth and industrialization. Growing domestic dissatisfaction with India's sluggish growth, ideational changes in economic-development strategies in other parts of the world, and the rise of the fast-growing economies of East and Southeast Asia all contributed to the reassessment of India's economic-growth model. However, it was not until an unprecedented fiscal crisis in 1991 that India undertook a fundamental shift in its economic policies. The results of these policies proved to be nothing short of dramatic. India managed to end its anemic rate of economic growth and started to make a dent in rural and urban poverty.

The profound changes that are sweeping across the Indian polity are also reflected in its foreign and security policies. Until Indian forces suffered a disastrous defeat at the hands of the Chinese People's Liberation Army (PLA) in 1962, Prime Minister Jawaharlal Nehru had deliberately limited defense spending and kept the Indian military on a short leash. Three related concerns had animated his defense policy. First, he had feared that an inordinate emphasis on military spending could lead to the militarization of Indian society. Second, he believed that military spending would impose significant opportunity costs that the nascent country could ill-afford. Third, he was concerned about the dangers of Bonapartism.

In the aftermath of the disastrous Sino-Indian border war India was compelled to increase defense spending dramatically. However, even though the war left Nehru a spent and broken man, the commitment to nonalignment remained. In later years, especially under Prime Minister Indira Gandhi, the country drew increasingly closer to the Soviet Union. The reasons for this shift are discussed at length in the chapter about foreign policy (see Chapter 2). Suffice it to say that the alignment with the Soviet Union stemmed mostly from geopolitical exigencies rather than any profound ideological affinity.

This reliance on the Soviets started to undergo a slow but steady shift during the early 1980s for a complex set of reasons. The Soviets were not in a position to provide India with the technologies that it needed for boosting economic growth, India was disenchanted with the Soviet invasion of Afghanistan, and the United States, under the Reagan administration, made important overtures toward India. However, it was not until the Cold War's end that India, for all practical purposes, abandoned the practice if not the rhetoric of nonalignment.

The Political Backdrop of the Past

A brief sketch of the political backdrop that preceded these revolutionary changes is in order. Prime Minister Nehru, in a schoolmasterly fashion, had encouraged parliamentary debate, maintained internal democracy within the Congress Party, continued the British tradition of a politically neutral civil service, fostered judicial independence, encouraged press freedom, boosted secularism, and firmly entrenched civilian control over the military.

Despite this extraordinary legacy, decay soon set in. Under Prime Minister Indira Gandhi much of the democratic and secular scaffolding that Nehru had so carefully constructed was taken down. Under her watch, the Congress Party's local roots withered, elections became increasingly plebiscitary, the independence of the judiciary was undermined, the principles of federalism were flouted, the civil service was politicized, and secularism was compromised. Her most destructive contribution, however, was the increasing personalization of politics and the deinstitutionalization of the polity. The Congress Party, a remarkable umbrella organization and a vibrant microcosm of Indian society, simply ossified.

As she dismantled the Congress Party, Gandhi also resorted to a series of populist gestures in an effort to garner personal popularity. She nationalized banks, dispensed with the annual payments to India's former royal families, and promised to abolish poverty. In the process, she raised the expectations of the poor and the disenfranchised and boosted their political mobilization. It was also under her tenure that India experienced its only bout of authoritarian "emergency" rule (1975–6), when civil liberties were suspended and personal rights squelched. The harshness of the brief authoritarian interlude led to an ironic comeuppance for Gandhi, however, as it was the very poor – whom she had mobilized – who used their newly invigorated franchise to oust her from office in 1977.

She would later return as prime minister, only to be assassinated by her own Sikh bodyguards in 1984. The democratic institutions that had survived her machinations also survived her demise. Her son and successor, the untried Rajiv Gandhi, did not consciously seek to worsen his mother's infelicitous legacy but did little to reverse it either. Deep-seated forces and powerful personalities in the Congress Party blocked his feeble efforts at reform. Once the mainstay of national unity, the Congress Party continued its steep decline, and political life began to fragment along regional and caste lines. Ethnoreligious conflicts in the Punjab and Kashmir intensified, and the federal features of the Indian polity, already parlous, became even more threadbare because of Rajiv's ill-considered policies.

His efforts did not stop with politics. His limited and over-cautious economic-reform efforts – meant to free an economy that had been brought to its knees by the all-stultifying weight of what the eminent Indian economist Raj Krishna called the "license, permit, quota raj" – ran afoul of powerful interests.[1] Career bureaucrats, fearing the loss of political prerogatives, dug in their heels against the implementation of reforms. Labor activists and their political allies led street protests. Businessmen who had grown rich in the statist hothouse showed scant hunger for more competition. Bereft of imagination and intestinal fortitude, Rajiv let reform lapse.

His May 1991 assassination by a Sri Lankan suicide bomber and the subsequent convergence of a series of political and economic forces, internal and external, brutally laid bare many of the structural weaknesses of the Indian polity. His killing came almost at the end of the Cold War, during the last two decades of which India had fashioned a cozy arms-transfer and security relationship with the Soviet Union, all the while professing a firm commitment to nonalignment. After the Soviet Union's collapse, Russia showed little interest in continuing the relationship on its previous basis. Consequently, Indian foreign- and security-policy makers abruptly found themselves adrift in a new and uncertain world.

The Cold War's end not only undermined the foundations of India's foreign policy but also helped to dissolve any consensus regarding economic growth and performance. Swelling deficits, rising oil prices, and the need to repatriate the more than one million overseas Indian workers whose jobs had been interrupted by the Iraqi invasion of Kuwait and the Gulf War exposed the Indian state to an ineluctable fiscal crisis. The long-sheltered, state-dominated economy, already smothered in regulations, now faced a huge challenge that was intellectual as well as practical. The Soviet collapse had robbed India's dirigiste bureaucrats and economists of what seemed to be a viable model for state-led economic growth. In a stroke of good fortune, however, the new prime minister and Congress Party stalwart, Narasimha Rao, and his Oxford University–trained finance minister, Manmohan Singh, had

---

[1] Meredith Woo Cummings, ed., *The Developmental State* (Ithaca, NY: Cornell University Press, 1999), 334.

the wit to seize upon the crisis as a potent lever against statism. Instead of seeking short-term loans as a safe harbor in a storm, they cut the cables that had bound the Indian economy to its old intellectual and institutional anchors and set a course for economic transformation.

Renewal and Reform

Despite the success of the Rao-Singh team in reversing the country's disastrous economic course, the Congress Party's political fortunes kept sliding. The reasons were structural; Indira Gandhi had let the party ossify, and no successor could or would repair the damage. Rajiv and Rao, for example, showed an anemic commitment to intraparty democracy and allowed significant corruption – ranging from illegal payments for government contracts to the bribing of legislators to defect before crucial votes – to go unchecked. Finally, despite their official commitment to secularism, the Congress Party's leaders showed little zeal in its defense. In 1985, for example, Rajiv overturned a Supreme Court judgment that provided a maintenance allowance to an indigent Muslim widow because he feared a backlash from Muslim clerics angered by the court's decision that Indian civil legislation should take precedence over Islamic law in this case. Later, in 1992, the Rao administration shamefully failed to stop Hindu-nationalist supporters of the BJP and its affiliate, the militant RSS, from tearing down the Babri Masjid, a mosque said to be have been constructed on the ruins of a Hindu temple. Worse still, the Rao government proved singularly inept at quelling the anti-Muslim riots that swept across India in the wake of the mosque's destruction.

The Congress Party's losses turned out to be the regional parties' gains. These formations, representing a wide array of local interests across the subcontinent, increasingly began to draw votes away from the Congress Party among India's hitherto disenfranchised minorities, whom the ruling party

regulations. The continuation of Seshan's innovations suggests that they were not the refulgent yet transitory attainments of one strong-willed man, but rather solid achievements that bespeak of a lasting improvement in the conduct of elections.[2] Thus, despite the decline and decay of a number of institutions, the renewal of other constitutionally mandated bodies such as the Supreme Court and the Election Commission bodes well for the future of Indian democracy.

Finally, the Right to Information Act has also bolstered the prospects of democratic governance in India. This act now empowers citizens to seek information regarding general government expenditures, inquire about arrears in pensions, seek information about spending on roads and public works, and ensure the delivery of various public services. The act, though quite extraordinary in terms of its scope and reach, has not always been implemented with great vigor. On many occasions bureaucrats have sought to intimidate individuals seeking information and have sought to obfuscate matters. Nevertheless, the act can play a significant role in increasing transparency and induce the bureaucracy to be more responsive to public needs.[3]

The Emergence of a New Social Order

In addition to the fitful renewal of political institutions, a fundamental transformation of India's social order is under way, with implications pointing in two directions: one promising for democracy, the other not. The salubrious development involves the mobilization of India's lower castes and minorities. Efforts to promote voter education and turnout, rising

[2] M. S. Gill, "India: Running the World's Biggest Elections," *Journal of Democracy* 9:1 (January 1998): 164–8.
[3] Alasdair S. Roberts, "A Great and Revolutionary Law? The First Four Years of India's Right to Information Act," *Suffolk University Law School Research Paper*, No. 10–02 (2010).

literacy rates, and widening exposure to mass media have promoted the effective enfranchisement of an ever-larger segment of India's population. Today, more poor Indians than
ever before know the power of the ballot box. Systematic
evidence exists that members of the lower-middle classes
take the franchise more seriously than do their complacent
middle-class compatriots.

The Question of Secularism

A less felicitous development has accompanied this dramatic
political mobilization: the burgeoning antisecular sentiment
in the country. Ironically, secularism is under attack from left-
wing intellectuals and right-wing ideologues. The Left has
attacked secularism on the grounds that it lacks an organic
basis in a fundamentally religious society. It contends that an
ethic of religious tolerance may be more appropriate than
secularism in the Indian context.

The right wing contends that Hinduism is not merely a
religion but an entire cultural ethos that pervades Indian life
and society. Consequently, it argues, a secular order is well-nigh
impossible in India. It also contends that secularism, as practiced
in India, has amounted to little more than the "pampering" of
minorities and is therefore "pseudosecularism."

Despite attacks on it from both ideological flanks, the
constitutional edifice of secularism still stands. How these
principles are actually enacted in everyday life is another
matter. There is no denying that Muslims and other minorities face various forms of discrimination in a range of social
and institutional interactions. Nevertheless, the preservation
of the constitutional apparatus of secularism is not a trivial
accomplishment.

The real danger that Indian secularism now faces stems from
the BJP's ability to transform the terms of political discourse
within India. Thanks to its antisecular rhetoric, the willingness of the BJP and its allies to resort to extraparliamentary

protests, and its ability to manipulate culturally sensitive issues, the texture of Indian politics has been significantly altered. Consequently, even professedly secular political parties like the Congress Party have felt compelled to make nods to anti-secular sentiments because of electoral exigencies. Thus, the long-term future of Indian secularism remains in abeyance as it confronts challenges from multiple quarters.

The Economic Transformation

The future of Indian secularism may well be fraught with uncertainty. However, there is no gainsaying that India has entered a wholly new economic arena. The economic transformation that is under way in India is nothing short of revolutionary.[4] Despite having strong credentials as political democrats, when it came to economics Jawaharlal Nehru and his lieutenants were unabashed statists in love with the idea that they could use government to reduce inequality, promote industrial transformation, and spur economic growth. In an age when the use of state power to secure such things seems far more dubious, it is important to recognize that India did achieve a degree of industrialization through state-led policies. State intervention in the economy was not an utterly futile enterprise.

Nevertheless, the kind and degree of state intervention mattered. As a number of scholars have shown, state intervention in India, unlike in East Asia, was needlessly and overly dirigiste, favoring "custodialism" over "husbandry."[5]

---

[4] Arvind Subramaniam, *India's Turn: Understanding the Economic Transformation* (New York: Oxford University Press, 2008).
[5] On the East Asian experience with economic growth, see Robert Wade, *Governing the Market: Economic Theory and the Role of Government in East Asia's Industrialization* (Princeton, NJ: Princeton University Press, 1990); also see Alice H. Amsden, *Asia's Next Giant: South Korea and Late Industrialization* (New York: Oxford University Press, 1989). On the contrast between custodialism and husbandry, see Peter B. Evans, *Embedded Autonomy: States and Industrial Transformation* (Princeton, NJ: Princeton University Press, 1995).

Not content with prudent efforts to encourage new industries, and thereby creating comparative advantage, the Indian government insisted on limiting the entry of firms into particular sectors, placing arcane and arbitrary limits on industrial and commercial expansion, and legislating labor regulations that stifled productivity. In pursuit of an import-substituting industrialization regime, it adopted extraordinarily autarkic economic policies, dramatically curtailing imports, imposing the highest tariff levels anywhere in the democratic world, and severely curbing the outward remittances of foreign exchange.

In time, the "winners" who benefited from this development strategy dug in to defend it. Businessmen came to rely on permits and quotas. Bureaucrats in New Delhi and in state capitals doled these out in accordance with the dictates of Soviet-style plans and, all too frequently, on the basis of clientelism. Because the system put a lid on competition, Indian industry had little reason to innovate, make quality improvements, or otherwise deliver more value to its customers.

Complex labor regulations enabled the growth of powerful and heavily politicized labor unions. Tied to political parties and almost exclusively confined to the organized sector of Indian industry, these organizations came to wield enormous clout. The restrictions on layoffs that they forced, although obviously good for their existing members, helped choke off productivity gains.

Finally, the Indian state, in a well-meaning but misguided attempt at pursuing egalitarian goals, fashioned a tax structure that encouraged evasion. During the initial years after independence, because rural poverty and shortages of food appeared endemic, no agricultural income was taxed. Even after commercial farming began to replace subsistence agriculture across large swaths of India, no politician wanted to face the wrath of the small-farmers' lobbies. Worse still, big farmers had gotten used to subsidized fertilizer and electricity, to say nothing of virtually free access to water. By the late 1980s, these giveaways were threatening to bankrupt the federal exchequer.

The 1991 crisis, as we have seen, provided an important opportunity for a decisive break with dirigisme. Although the past decade has seen considerable political instability and repeated cabinet turnovers, most commentators insist that the reforms begun under Rao and Singh are now irreversible. There is, however, continuing debate about the scope, degree, and pace of the reforms but not over their basic nature or direction. A full assessment of these reforms and their impact can be found in the chapter on the economic revolution (see Chapter 3).

The Military Strategic Revolution

The profound changes sweeping across the Indian polity are also reflected in its foreign and security policies. These changes are not bereft of domestic implications for the future of democratic governance. Until Indian forces were routed in the tragic 1962 border war with China, Nehru had deliberately limited defense spending and kept the military on a short leash. Three related concerns had animated his policy. First, he worried that too much emphasis on military spending would lead to the pervasive militarization of Indian society. Second, he believed that military spending would entail significant opportunity costs that a poor, young nation could ill-afford. Third, he feared that a large military establishment might create propitious conditions for a neo-Bonapartist "man on horseback."

Thus, Nehru opted for his famous policy of nonalignment, seeking to steer a middle course between two emergent global power blocs led by the Soviet Union and the United States, respectively. This policy was accompanied by an aversion to the use of force in international affairs, a desire to see the abolition of nuclear weapons, a strong tendency to support decolonization, and an advocacy of multilateralism in diplomacy. Inevitably, as with any ideological formulation, there was a gap between the goals professed and the practices followed. For instance, India was compelled to resort to arms against Pakistan almost immediately after independence and then again in 1965 and 1971. In an effort to counter what was perceived in New Delhi as an emergent Sino-American strategic nexus, India forged a quasi-alliance with the Soviet Union in 1971, thereby fundamentally compromising its credentials as a nonaligned nation. After the 1962 Sino-Indian border war, India embarked on a significant military buildup. In the aftermath of the 1971 war with Pakistan, India started to speed up its nascent, covert nuclear-weapons program.

The Cold War's end rendered the concept of nonalignment meaningless and swept away whatever vestiges had remained of India's notion of a foreign policy. Simultaneously, India quickly discovered Russia's lack of interest in guaranteeing India's security against threats from China. Nor was Russia willing to keep selling India highly sophisticated military equipment at bargain rates. This seismic shift in the regional security environment forced India's leaders to make new strategic calculations. Not surprisingly, they made a concerted effort to improve relations with the United States, a country that India had viewed with considerable suspicion and distrust throughout much of the Cold War. They also resumed their efforts to improve relations with China while devoting adequate resources to the maintenance of a resolute and robust military posture to cope with any renewed threat.

The most significant shift, however, came about in India's attitude toward the role and utility of nuclear weapons. The end of the Cold War had engendered hopes in India regarding the possibility of shrinking the nuclear gyre. These hopes quickly proved to be chimerical as the five recognized nuclear powers, despite pious professions of reducing their reliance on nuclear weapons, artfully strove to preserve and sanctify their nuclear monopoly through a complex web of multilateral treaty arrangements. Fearing that their security would now be at considerable risk, especially in the face of an economically resurgent and militarily assertive China, Indian decision makers fundamentally reassessed the security environment that their country faced. The rise of a more conservative and jingoistic political party, the BJP, certainly facilitated such a recalculation. Not surprisingly, shortly after the BJP's ascent to power in 1998, its leaders decided to cross the nuclear Rubicon, despite the certain prospect of economic sanctions and widespread political disapprobation from the great powers. Since then, despite a change of regime in New Delhi, the nuclear-weapons program has proceeded apace.

The Future of Democratic India

Will the dream of a democratic, secular, and prosperous India endure? Despite the significant challenges confronting the nation, it appears that Indian democracy will survive and thrive despite the myriad threats that face it. Such optimism is not unwarranted. The logic of economic liberalization is working in favor of a deeper and fuller federalism. As the enthusiasm for centralized economic interventionism continues to wane, the power of national government in New Delhi shrinks and power over economic and fiscal policy shifts to state capitals in a process that dovetails neatly with the regionalization of politics in the post–Congress Party era.

The upsurge of popular participation, especially on the part of the lower castes and minorities, should help check the more egregious attacks on secularism. The BJP can relentlessly pursue the Hindutva agenda only at the cost of alienating numerous lower-caste voters in the populous Hindi-speaking belt of northern India. Simultaneously, the need to maintain coalition allies, many of whom represent diverse constituencies, should also curb some of the more extreme propensities of the BJP and its affiliates such as the RSS.

What about economic prosperity? It is safe to assume that no Indian government will seek a full-blown return to the country's statist economy four decades after independence. Yet it would be premature to suggest that this sea of change in the economic-policy consensus means that the requisite political forces are in place to sustain rapid reform. Combinations of unions, businessmen clinging to rent seeking and high tariffs, state-sector workers worried about their jobs, bureaucrats jealous of their prerogatives, and politicians eyeing the next election will attempt to staff the reform process. Only a moderately secure regime in New Delhi can overcome their opposition and keep India on the path to prosperity.

Finally, will the quest for nuclear weapons and an enhanced appreciation of the importance of national security undermine India's fiscal stability, corrode the established pattern of civil-military relations, and contribute to the militarization of Indian society? All these fears, though often expressed, are largely groundless. Despite India's overt nuclearization and the renewed emphasis on national security, the average annual spending on defense still stands at less than 5 percent of the gross national product – an entirely feasible allocation that a far less wealthy India long managed to sustain without draining its exchequer.[6] Nor is the supremacy of elected officials over the military under any threat, despite the emerging organizational needs of fashioning and maintaining a small, secure nuclear arsenal. The final control of these weapons remains in civilian hands, and the military continues to respect this institutional arrangement. The normative ballast that these organizational procedures have developed during a span of sixty years also suggests that the existing order of civil-military relations will endure with minor and appropriate modifications.

In the face of myriad challenges, democracy in India has survived and has grown deep roots in the country's soil. Despite India's failure to promote rapid economic development and abolish abject poverty, the country can be justifiably proud of having sustained a democratic order. As the world confronts a host of violent, atavistic, and chiliastic movements, the success of India's democratic polity offers a modicum of hope for the new century.

[6] Laxman Kumar Behera, "India's Affordable Defense Spending," *Journal of Defence Studies* 2:1 (Summer 2008): 136–48.

2

The Transformation of India's Foreign Policy

The Past as Prologue

From the vantage point of the Cold War's end, India's pursuit of a foreign policy based upon nonalignment now appears quaint at best and hypocritical at worst. It appears quaint because after its initial phase the policy ill-served India's interest and appears hypocritical because the country often failed to live up to its cherished principles. This was especially true after it signed a treaty of "peace, friendship and cooperation" with the Soviet Union effectively aligning India with the Soviet Union.[1] Yet some understanding of the historical context that spawned the doctrine reveals that it was not bereft of utility to India's national interests.

Prime Minister Nehru, who was the principal architect of independent India's foreign policy, had fashioned this doctrine for a number of compelling reasons.[2] Perhaps the most compelling were the memories of British colonial domination.[3]

[1] For a discussion and analysis of the politics underlying the treaty see Surinder Nihal Singh, *The Yogi and the Bear* (Riverdale, NY: Riverdale Company, 1988).

[2] For an important argument that holds that Nehru's role in the formulation of an independent India's foreign policy has been overstated, see T. A. Keenleyside, "The Inception of Indian Foreign Policy: The Non-Nehru Contribution," *South Asia: Journal of South Asian Studies* 4:2 (1982): 63–78.

[3] His views can be gleaned from Jawaharlal Nehru, *The Discovery of India* (Oxford: Oxford University Press, 1990).

Consequently, the notion of subordinating the nascent country's foreign policy to the interests and proclivities of either emergent superpower bloc was repugnant. Nehru was also acutely concerned about the possibilities of Bonapartism and the militarization of Indian society.[4] Associating India with one of the two power blocs could, in his view, lead India to divert its scarce resources toward unwanted military spending. Finally, nonalignment was also part of a larger strategy to transform the global order. Nehru and others had hoped that it would contribute to the strength of multilateral fora, hobble the use of force in international politics, reduce global inequalities, and bring an end to the last remnants of colonialism.[5] Apart from India's useful role as a mediating force in Korea and Laos the only arena in which the nonaligned movement had any impact was in delegitimizing colonialism.[6]

By the time of Nehru's death in 1964, nonalignment was losing much of its early sheen. China had attacked India in 1962, and few of the nonaligned states evinced any interest in condemning its action.[7] Indian policy makers, most notably Nehru, had been forced to abandon their deeply held hopes of limiting defense expenditures. Within a year of the Chinese invasion, India had practically doubled its defense expenditures as a percentage of its gross domestic product (GDP).[8] It had also embarked upon a major military-modernization program including the creation of a million-man army; ten new

---

[4] On these dangers, see Sumit Ganguly, "From the Defense of the Nation to Aid to the Civil: The Army in Contemporary India," *Journal of Asian and African Affairs* 26 (1991): 1–12.

[5] For a trenchant and thoughtful critique of the practice of nonalignment, see Fouad Ajami, "The Third World Challenge: The Fate of Nonalignment," *Foreign Affairs* 59:2 (1980–1): 366–85.

[6] On the Indian role in Korea, see D. R. Sardesai, *Indian Foreign Policy in Cambodia, Laos, and Vietnam, 1947–1964* (Berkeley: University of California Press, 1968).

[7] On the origins of the Sino-Indian border war, see Steven Hoffman, *India and the China Crisis* (Berkeley: University of California Press, 1990).

[8] Raju G. C. Thomas, *The Defense of India: A Budgetary Perspective on Strategy and Politics* (New York: Macmillan, 1978).

mountain divisions equipped and trained for mountain war-
fare; a forty-five-squadron air force equipped with modern,
supersonic aircraft; and a modest naval-expansion program.[9]

Not long after Nehru's death and the first Chinese nuclear
tests, his successor, Lal Bahadur Shastri, embarked upon a
modest but dedicated nuclear-weapons program.[10] Indira
Gandhi, Nehru's daughter, who succeeded Shastri, continued
to rely on the language of nonalignment. However, one of
its principal tenets, the attempt to hobble the use of force in
international relations, appeared no longer to be a guiding
principle of India's foreign policy.

Apart from its commitment to a global redistribution of
resources, which India espoused in a loose organization –
the Group of Seventy-Seven (G-77) – and an anticolonial
impulse, few if any, of the original commitments of nonalignment continued to undergird or animate India's foreign-
policy concerns.[11] In spite of this, India provided diplomatic
and rhetorical support for the last anti-Portuguese movements
in Angola and Mozambique in order to oppose the apartheid
regime in South Africa staunchly and provide political support to the Palestinians.

This chapter will focus on the transformation of India's foreign policy since 1980. It will show that despite the limitations
of a commitment to some variant of nonalignment, structural
constraints prevented a dramatic shift in India's foreign policy.
It will also argue that only a fundamental transformation of the
global order after the Cold War initially induced India's policy
makers to reorder the country's priorities. Subsequently, the
policies became less reactive. The chapter is also divided into
three distinct sections. It focuses on relations with the Soviet

[9] Lorne J. Kavic, *India's Quest for Security: Defence Policies, 1947–1965*
(Berkeley: University of California Press, 1967).

[10] Ashok Kapur, *India's Nuclear Option: Atomic Diplomacy and Decision
Making* (New York: Praeger, 1976).

[11] For a discussion of the use of multilateral organizations to try and bring
about a global redistribution of wealth, see Steven Krasner, *Structural
Conflict: The Third World against Global Liberalism* (Berkeley: University of
California Press, 1985).

Union (and then its principal successor state, Russia) and the United States, India's two principal adversaries (Pakistan and China), and Southeast Asia. It does not purport to provide a complete and thorough account of Indian foreign policy during this period. However, it does emphasize the interplay of structure and agency in order to highlight critical turning points. Though every effort will be made to keep these discussions analytically and substantively discrete, a degree of overlap is inevitable.

The Soviet Invasion of Afghanistan: An Intersection of Key Interests

In December 1979, the Soviet Union invaded Afghanistan.[12] The Soviet invasion of a South Asian country presented a unique dilemma for India's policy makers. Indian policy makers correctly feared that the Soviet intrusion would almost inevitably bring superpower rivalry into the region. More to the point, they accurately surmised that Pakistan, their principal adversary, would align with the United States in attempts to counter the Soviet presence in Afghanistan. This would entail providing the Pakistani military dictatorship of General Zia-ul-Haq substantial military assistance thereby altering the military balance on the subcontinent, one that had favored India since Pakistan's dramatic military defeat in 1971.[13]

Since 1971, India had forged a formal security relationship with the Soviet Union. Under the aegis of this treaty, India had become a major recipient of Soviet military largesse.[14] Such assistance had enabled India to become the predominant

---

[12] The literature on the Soviet invasion of Afghanistan is voluminous. A useful sample is Henry Bradsher, *Afghanistan and the Soviet Union* (Durham, NC: Duke University Press, 1985).

[13] For a description and analysis of the various Indo-Pakistani conflicts, see Sumit Ganguly, *Conflict Unending: India-Pakistan Tensions since 1947* (New York: Columbia University Press, 2001).

[14] See the discussion in Robert Horn, *Soviet-Indian Relations: Issues and Influence* (New York: Praeger, 1982).

military power in the region. Such military dominance had also ensured a period of relative peace in Indo-Pakistani relations. It had also conferred sufficient confidence on India's policy makers to enable them to start discussions with the People's Republic of China for the resolution of a long-standing border dispute that had culminated in a brutal war in 1962.[15]

The invasion also came at a particularly inopportune moment for India's domestic politics. Prime Minister Indira Gandhi had just been reelected to office following the disarray of the Janata Dal–led regime.[16] However, she was yet to assume office formally, and the interim government of Prime Minister Chaudhuri Charan Singh, a regional leader elevated to this position, was in office. An interim regime could not make binding decisions for India's foreign and security policies; however, regardless of the individual or party in office, the Soviet invasion and occupation of Afghanistan presented a structural dilemma for India's leaders. Its military and security dependence on the Soviet Union was significant, and consequently, Indian policy makers could not publicly and unequivocally condemn the Soviet actions in Afghanistan without incurring considerable costs. Simultaneously, they realized that the Soviet intrusion into the region had suddenly transformed Pakistan from being a virtual pariah state to one of vital strategic significance to the United States. To elicit and obtain Pakistan's cooperation successfully in any anti-Soviet enterprise, the United States would be forced to bolster Pakistan's military capabilities to India's detriment.

A Tectonic Shift: The Cold War's End

It is hard to adequately discuss the significance of the Soviet demise and the end of the Cold War on India's foreign

---

[15] Hoffman, *India and the China Crisis.*

[16] She had previously been ousted from office in 1977 in the wake of new elections following her declaration of a "state of emergency" in 1975. For an analysis of the events that led to the declaration of the state of emergency and its aftermath, see Henry Hart, ed., *Indira Gandhi's India: A Political System Re-Appraised* (Boulder, CO: Westview Press, 1978).

policy.[17] A senior Indian diplomat, in a private conversation, once described the impact of the Soviet dissolution as the equivalent of the disappearance of a supernova.[18] Indian policy makers had seen the Indo-Soviet relationship as one of the cornerstones of their country's foreign and security policies. India had not only relied on the arms-transfer relationship, which had terms that were quite beneficial to the Indian exchequer, but had also counted on the Soviet Union for two critical matters. First, it had relied on the Soviet veto in the United Nations (UN) Security Council. The Soviets had twice used this veto to protect India from international censure during its intervention in the East Pakistan crisis that had culminated in the creation of Bangladesh. Later, India had come to count on it to prevent the Kashmir question from being raised at the UN Security Council. Second, India had also seen the Soviets as the guarantor of its security against possible Chinese revanchism. All these assurances, in a single fell swoop, disappeared virtually overnight.

This structural shift in power necessitated a fundamental reappraisal of India's foreign policy. Some commentators continued to hold out hope that the Nehruvian model was not bereft of significance despite these profound, systemic changes in global politics.[19] However, other observers argued that India needed to drastically change the orientation of its foreign policy and was in the process of making that shift.[20] This realignment of India's priorities and policy postures was

---

[17] For a slightly idiosyncratic but nevertheless insightful account, see C. Raja Mohan, *Crossing the Rubicon: The Shaping of India's New Foreign Policy* (New Delhi: Palgrave/Macmillan, 2003). For a general discussion of the impact of international politics on the domestic arrangements of states, see Peter Gourevitch, "The Second Image Reversed: The Domestic Consequences of International Politics," *International Organization* 32:4 (1978): 881–912.

[18] Personal interview with a senior Indian diplomat, New York City, October 1991.

[19] See, e.g., S. D. Muni, "India and the Post-Cold-War World: Opportunities and Challenges," *Asian Survey* 31:9 (1991): 862–74.

[20] For an early discussion, see Sumit Ganguly, "South Asia after the Cold War," *The Washington Quarterly* 15:4 (1992): 173–84.

most evident in six regions, and involved a steady warming of relations with Israel; a concomitant end to uncritical support for the Palestinian question; a gradual and, subsequently, significant transformation of Indo-U.S. relations; the crossing of the nuclear Rubicon in 1998; a fitful and cautious attempt to alter the tenor of Sino-Indian relations; the maintenance of a limited but important arms-transfer relationship with Russia; and a concerted effort to make inroads into Southeast Asia.

An End to Indo-Arab Solidarity?

The transformation of India's foreign policy toward the Middle East in general and Israel in particular merit special attention. Indian foreign-policy makers, in a sharp departure from long-standing policy and practice, chose to upgrade India's diplomatic relations with Israel in January 1992. This decision came shortly after India's vote to overturn the invidious 1975 UN resolution, which had equated Zionism with racism. India had cosponsored this resolution during the heyday of nonalignment and Third World solidarity.[21]

India had refused to have full diplomatic ties with Israel during the Cold War for two reasons. At one level, they wanted to demonstrate their solidarity with the Arab world and to express sympathy for the Palestinians. In considerable part, making common cause with the Arabs regarding the Palestinian conflict in turn stemmed from the anticolonial component of the nonalignment movement (NAM). At another level, support for the Palestinian cause assuaged the sentiments of significant segments of India's substantial Muslim minority. Ironically, when India moved ahead to grant full diplomatic status to Israel, the criticisms from external and domestic sources were quite muted.[22]

---

[21] P. R. Kumaraswamy, "India and Israel: An Emerging Partnership," in *India as an Emerging Power*, ed. Sumit Ganguly (London: Frank Cass and Company, 2003), 192–206.

[22] Ibid.

India chose to improve its diplomatic ties with Israel in order to pursue two distinct but related objectives. It wanted to improve relations with the United States. Indian policy makers calculated that Israel's close relationship with the United States would, in turn, enable them to help open the way to better relations with the United States. India also wanted to develop closer ties to Israel because the attempts to cultivate the Arab world for well more than thirty years had hindered India's strategic goals. For example, during all the Indo-Pakistani conflicts, the vast majority of the Arab states, including Egypt, one of the original members of NAM, had adopted an explicitly pro-Pakistani stance or had been disinterested bystanders at best.

Since the 1992 decision to grant full diplomatic recognition to Israel, the Indo-Israeli relationship has strengthened significantly. A Congress Party government, despite fears of a backlash in the Arab world and in the substantial Muslim community within India, had ended India's diplomatic isolation of Israel. The Bharatiya Janata Party (BJP)–led coalition that came to power in 1998 did not share any such compunctions. They had long argued for the granting of full diplomatic status to Israel, and consequently they expanded the scope of defense, security, and economic cooperation. Given the BJP's hostility toward Pakistan and its preoccupation with Islamist terror, it also expanded the scope and dimensions of its counterterrorism cooperation with Israel. Despite the return of a Congress Party–led government in 2004, Indo-Israeli cooperation has shown little or no sign of slackening. Common interests in economic, military, and counterterrorism cooperation have cemented this relationship. Even Israel's harsh, punitive expedition into Lebanon during July 2006 did not elicit any sharp disapprobation from Indian official quarters. During the Cold War years, any such military venture would have resulted in much official upbraiding and widespread public recriminations.[23]

---

[23] P. R. Kumaraswamy, *India's Israel Policy* (New York: Columbia University Press, 2010).

India and Pakistan: The Abortive Quest for a Regional Solution

At least a decade prior to the Cold War's end, the Soviet invasion of Afghanistan had dramatic consequences for Indo-Pakistani relations, regional stability, and the future of Indo-U.S. relations. Unfortunately, much of the commentary regarding India's stance on the Soviet invasion is polemical, partisan, and misleading.[24] Contrary to most popular accounts, which rely on India's bland public stance on the Soviet invasion at the UN General Assembly, the Indian response to the Soviet invasion was quite sophisticated. Immediately after the invasion, the interim Indian prime minister, Chaudhuri Charan Singh, called in the Soviet ambassador to New Delhi and delivered a rather sharp message of disapproval. Charan Singh, though a regional politician, was astute enough to understand the adverse regional ramifications of the Soviet invasion.[25] Even after his brief tenure in office ended, Prime Minister Indira Gandhi, who was widely (and correctly) seen as being pro-Soviet, despite adopting a publicly anodyne position toward the Soviet Union, pursued a more complex and nuanced private diplomatic strategy. In private communications with the Soviets she expressed her displeasure over the invasion. Additionally, she dispatched her trusted minister for external affairs, Narasimha Rao, to Islamabad in early 1980. Narasimha Rao's brief was clear: India would not seek to exploit Pakistan's adverse security situation if it chose not to draw the United States into the region.[26] This effort, a strategy of reassurance, proved to be fruitless.[27] Zia and the

---

[24] For an especially thoughtful and dispassionate assessment, see Robert C. Horn, "Afghanistan and the Soviet-Indian Influence Relationship," *Asian Survey* 23:3 (March 1983): 244–60.

[25] Based upon a personal interview with a senior Indian diplomat, New York City, October 1992.

[26] On this point, see Bhabani Sen Gupta, *The Afghan Syndrome: How to Live with Soviet Power* (London: Croom Helm, 1982).

[27] For a discussion of the concept of reassurance, see Andrew H. Kydd, *Trust and Mistrust in International Relations* (Princeton, NJ: Princeton University Press, 2005).

Pakistani military's intransigence toward India, the deep sense of distrust of Indian intentions, and the possibility of substantial American largesse all conspired against the quest for an imaginative regional response to the Soviet invasion.[28]

Pakistan chose to align itself with the United States in the quest for substantial military assistance. Pakistan's choice proved to bring considerable largesse. During the next five years the United States provided Pakistan the sum of $3.2 billion in military and economic assistance. Subsequently, it gave Pakistan another tranche of assistance amounting to $4.02 billion over the course of six years. (The second tranche, however, was not fully delivered because the Afghan conflict came to a close with the Soviet withdrawal in 1990 and the United States imposed severe sanctions on Pakistan under the aegis of the Pressler Amendment.)[29]

In an effort to buttress its relationship with India, the Soviet Union made every effort to provide it with the weaponry that New Delhi sought in order to offset Pakistani weapons acquisitions. Accordingly, it readily provided India with substantial quantities of sophisticated military equipment including the MiG-29 during the Afghanistan war years.[30] Indian decision makers, although unhappy with the Soviet presence in Afghanistan, nevertheless adopted a most anodyne public position regarding the Soviet occupation. Their posture at one level was undoubtedly hypocritical. India could ill-afford to continue to champion nonalignment while maintaining a mostly studied public silence on the Soviet invasion and brutal occupation of a sovereign state.

---

[28] Despite the failure of this initial overture, influential Indians continued to promote the significance of possible regional solutions. On this subject, see the perceptive essay by Jagat Mehta, a former Indian foreign secretary, "Afghanistan: A Neutral Solution," *Foreign Policy* 47:3 (Summer 1982): 139–53.

[29] The Pressler Amendment, after Senator Larry Pressler (Republican–South Dakota), made aid contingent on the U.S. president stating that Pakistan did "not possess a nuclear explosive device."

[30] On this subject, see Linda Racioppi, *Soviet Policy towards South Asia since 1970* (Cambridge: Cambridge University Press, 1994).

Yet its leaders, whether Indira Gandhi or her son and successor, Rajiv Gandhi, saw few viable alternatives to India's
continued reliance on the Soviet Union. Certain structural constraints at the level of both the international and
the regional systems placed important limitations on India's
maneuverability. At the global level, the United States, under
the Reagan administration, given its visceral anti-Communist
orientation and its unyielding outlook toward Soviet mal-
feasance, had evinced no interest in the pursuit of a regional
solution. Instead, they had chosen to overlook all the myriad shortcomings of Pakistan's internal political arrangements
and had decided to work with the Zia regime in order to
find a mostly military solution. India's concerns and sentiments had been of little concern to American policy makers in the Reagan administration who saw the world in
Manichean terms when it came to dealing with the Soviet
Union.[31] Consequently, India could not turn to the United
States to address its continuing and compelling security concerns stemming from Pakistan and China.

At a regional level, India's room for maneuver was also limited. Relations with the People's Republic of China (PRC)
had not improved significantly despite Prime Minister
Vajpayee's visit to Beijing in 1976. Moreover, China was now
clearly aligned with the United States and had a decidedly
anti-Soviet orientation. Under these circumstances, Indian
policy makers had little or no interest in attempting to alter
the course of India's principal foreign-policy alignments.

Finally, domestic political arrangements also inhibited
India from changing course. They merely reinforced the
existing structural constraints at global and regional levels. As
discussed later in this chapter, Indira Gandhi and her close
advisers had serious doubts about the reliability of the United
States as a potential partner, which stemmed from a variety

---

[31] Raymond Garthoff, *Détente and Confrontation: American-Soviet Relations
from Nixon to Reagan* (Washington, DC: Brookings Institution, 1985).

of experiences, most notably those under the Johnson and Nixon administrations.[32]

This renewed American involvement with Pakistan initially contributed to a more distant relationship with the United States and to greater tensions with Pakistan. Prime Minister Indira Gandhi had come to view the United States with considerable suspicion because of its role in supporting Pakistan during the 1971 Bangladesh crisis. Apart from a limited breakthrough that occurred at Cancun, Mexico, when Indira Gandhi met with Ronald Reagan at a North-South summit, Indo-U.S. relations remained frosty. No serious attempts at improving relations would take place until after her assassination in 1984 and the ascendance of Rajiv Gandhi.

Rajiv Gandhi and the Limits of Rapprochement

Indira Gandhi's death in 1984 at the hands of her Sikh bodyguards led the Congress Party to rally around her son, Rajiv Gandhi, a former airline pilot and a political neophyte. A number of complex reasons explain India's failure to change its foreign-policy orientation under Rajiv Gandhi. First, he had no substantial political experience when he entered office. Consequently, he was acutely reliant on the advice of trusted acolytes of his mother and those within the Congress Party. Second, India still faced certain structural constraints. When he assumed office in 1984, the Cold War was at its apogee thanks to the Soviet presence in Afghanistan and the unyielding anti-Communist posture of the Reagan administration.[33] In turn, the Reagan administration had embraced Pakistan as the linchpin of its strategy to dislodge the Soviets from Afghanistan. Under these circumstances, few Indian leaders would be comfortable in making a fundamental shift in foreign policy.

---

[32] See the discussions in Surjit Mansingh, *India's Quest for Power: Indira Gandhi's Foreign Policy* (New Delhi: Sage Publications, 1982).

[33] On this subject, see Garthoff, *Détente and Confrontation*.

Continuing Tensions

Throughout the decade of the 1980s Indo-Pakistani relations continued to deteriorate. Once again, global and regional trends proved to be mutually reinforcing. At a global level, the United States, despite minor overtures toward India, continued to bolster the military regime in Pakistan. From a parochial standpoint, American policy made sense. Given India's closeness to the Soviet Union and Pakistan's willingness to work with the United States to raise the costs of the Soviet occupation, American policy makers simply chose the most expedient strategy.

Pakistan, in turn, exploited the American preoccupation with Afghanistan to steadily build up its conventional forces and nuclear capabilities. American assistance contributed to the renewal of its conventional capabilities. Its nuclear arsenal was the result of self-help and Chinese assistance.[34] Throughout the decade, Indian policy makers watched these developments with growing alacrity and quietly speeded up their nuclear-weapons and ballistic-missile programs in response to Pakistan's expanding capabilities.

The growth in their respective capabilities and Pakistan's involvement in an ethnoreligious insurgency in the Indian border state of Punjab contributed, in the 1980s, to a series of crises that punctuated Indo-Pakistani relations.[35] The origins of the Punjab insurgency were indigenous and have been discussed elsewhere.[36] Suffice it to write that the origins of

[34] On the growth of the Pakistani nuclear-weapons program, as well as Chinese assistance, see Steven Weismann and Herbert Krosney, *The Islamic Bomb* (New York: Times Books, 1981). Also see Ashok Kapur, *Pakistan's Nuclear Development* (London: Routledge, 1987); Ziba Moshaver, *Nuclear Weapons Proliferation in the Indian Subcontinent* (New York: Palgrave, 1991).

[35] For a discussion of these crises, see Sumit Ganguly and Devin Hagerty, *Fearful Symmetry: India and Pakistan in the Shadow of Nuclear Weapons* (Seattle: University of Washington Press, 2004).

[36] See, e.g., Gurharpal Singh, *Ethnic Conflict in India: A Case-Study of Punjab* (New Delhi: Palgrave, 2000); Robin Jeffrey, *What's Happening to India?*

the Punjab insurgency were rooted in the historical legacy of the partition of India, the shortcomings of Indian federalism (especially under Indira Gandhi), and the concomitant rise of a violent revivalist movement in the region in the aftermath of the transformation of the socioeconomic landscape as a consequence of the green revolution.[37]

As the insurgency took root and posed a challenge to the unity of the Indian state, Pakistani decision makers quickly became involved in aiding and abetting the insurgents through the provision of arms, training, and above all, sanctuaries.[38] The growth of Pakistani military capabilities in conjunction with its feckless involvement in the Punjab insurgency caused increasing frustration in Indian security decision-making circles. The two concerns in concert led the Indian military to consider some drastic action against the Pakistani state. This culminated in what is known as the 1987 Brasstacks crisis. The crisis nearly resulted in another war because of mutual misperception, risk taking, and miscalculation.[39]

The immediate precipitants of the crisis can be traced to the decision of the Indian Army, under the leadership of Chief of Staff General Krishnaswami Sundarji, to conduct a military exercise of unprecedented size and scope in the Rajasthan desert adjoining the Pakistani province of Sindh along an East-West axis. No clear-cut evidence in the public domain

Punjab, Ethnic Conflict, Mrs. Gandhi's Death, and the Test for Federalism (New York: Holmes and Meyer, 1986); M. J. Akbar, *India: The Siege Within* (New York: Penguin Books, 1985).

[37] On the socioeconomic consequences of the green revolution, see Francine Frankel, *India's Green Revolution: Economic Gains and Political Costs* (Princeton, NJ: Princeton University Press, 1971).

[38] On Pakistani involvement in the Sikh insurgency, see Paul Wallace, "Political Violence and Terrorism in India: The Crisis of Identity," in *Terrorism in Context*, ed. Martha Crenshaw (University Park: Pennsylvania State University Press, 1994).

[39] Much of the discussion that follows is drawn from Kanti Bajpai, P. R. Chari, Pervez Iqbal Cheema, and Sumit Ganguly, *Brasstacks and Beyond: Perception and the Management of Crisis in South Asia* (New Delhi: Manohar, 1989).

exists that can link the decision to hold this potentially provocative military exercise with Pakistani involvement in the Punjab. However, there is sufficient circumstantial evidence to construct such a case based upon inference and attribution.[40]

It is beyond the scope of this chapter to discuss the evolution and termination of this crisis in any detail. Suffice it to state that it ended because the United States and then the Soviet Union played key roles in defusing tensions. The Brasstacks crisis underscored the role of a charismatic and risk-prone Chief of Army Staff who was able to persuade a neophyte prime minister into undertaking a major exercise in coercive diplomacy.

Despite the pursuit of a range of confidence-building measures developed in the wake of this crisis, the propensity of the Pakistani military to meddle in India's domestic politics remained constant. In the Punjab, when an opportunity arose, the Pakistani military regime had sought to manipulate and exacerbate an indigenous uprising and had, in considerable measure, met with success. When a similar opportunity presented itself in Kashmir, thanks to the many malfeasances of the Indian state, it wasted no time or effort to seize the day. This opportunity arose in 1989 when an ethnoreligious insurgency erupted in the disputed state of Jammu and Kashmir. The Pakistani politico-military establishment had previously tried unsuccessfully to foment a rebellion in the state.[41] This time, however, their efforts to stir the existing reservoir of discontent in Indian-controlled Kashmir met with considerable success.[42]

The crisis originated in the domestic politics of the Indian-controlled section of the state of Jammu and Kashmir.[43] The

[40] For an early discussion of the Brasstacks crisis, see Sumit Ganguly, "Getting Down to Brass Tacks," *The World and I* (May 1987): 100–4.

[41] Russell Brines, *The Indo-Pakistani Conflict* (New York: Pall Mall, 1968).

[42] On Pakistani support for the insurgency, see Daniel Byman, *Deadly Connections: States that Sponsor Terrorism* (New York: Cambridge University Press, 2005).

[43] The literature on the Kashmir crisis is vast. A small sampling includes Sumit Ganguly, *The Crisis in Kashmir: Portents of War, Hopes of Peace* (Cambridge:

insurgency began when the members of a Kashmiri separatist group, the Jammu and Kashmir Liberation Front (JKLF) kidnapped Rubaiya Sayeed, the daughter of then Union Minister for Home Affairs, Mufti Mohammed Sayeed, a Kashmiri Muslim politician. The coalition regime, which was in power in New Delhi, quickly acquiesced to the demands of the kidnappers in exchange for her release. The willingness of the regime in New Delhi to easily succumb to the demands of the insurgents had a dramatic emboldening effect on the perpetrators, their sympathizers, and other nascent separatist groups. Within weeks, a spate of bombings and attacks shook the Kashmir Valley. In its time-honored fashion, the Indian state initially sought to crush this latest rebellion with a mailed fist (harsh military response) despite caving into the initial demands of the JKLF.

Once again, even a civilian Pakistani regime under Prime Minister Benazir Bhutto could not avoid the temptation of promptly entering the fray on behalf of the indigenous insurgents. As a consequence of the prompt, generous, and targeted Pakistani support to the various insurgents, toward the spring of 1990 the valley was awash in violence. Indian security forces, despite their substantial experience with counterinsurgency operations elsewhere, could not maintain order let alone law in the region. Faced with this situation, Indian policy makers considered striking insurgent training camps within Pakistan. In the end, they chose not to carry out these air strikes because they feared the possibilities of escalation. Additionally, the Deputy U.S. National Security Adviser, Robert M. Gates, flew to Islamabad and New Delhi in the spring of 1990 seeking to defuse the impending crisis. In New Delhi he counseled restraint, and in Islamabad he warned the Pakistanis that all American war

Cambridge University Press, 1997); Victoria Schofield, *Kashmir in the Crossfire* (New York: I. B. Tauris, 1996); Raju G. C. Thomas, *Perspectives on Kashmir: The Roots of Conflict in South Asia* (Boulder, CO: Westview Press, 1992); Sten Widmalm, *Democracy and Violent Separatism in India: Kashmir in Comparative Perspective* (Oxford: Oxford University Press, 2002).

games showed that Pakistan would lose a conventional conflict with India.[44]

Though war was successfully avoided in Kashmir in 1990, the issue continued to fester and still bedevils Indo-Pakistani relations. Even the overt nuclearization of the region in 1998 did not lead to an abatement of the conflict. Instead, acquisition of a working nuclear arsenal emboldened Pakistan's decision makers to undertake a "limited probe"[45] in April 1999 in Kargil, a largely uninhabited and poorly defended part of the Indian-controlled section of Kashmir.[46]

Few Pakistani accounts of the Kargil crisis are available.[47] Consequently, it is difficult to articulate the precise goals that the leadership had in mind when they undertook this probe. However, through a process of inference and attribution it can be argued that the central goal was to refocus flagging international attention on the Kashmir question.[48] They had also made a fundamentally flawed assumption that the international community, and especially the United States, would necessarily assume a neutral position on the crisis, if not an overly pro-Pakistani stance.[49] All their assumptions proved to

---

[44] The precise impact of the Gates mission is unclear and the subject of a vigorous debate on the subcontinent. For a careful discussion, see Devin Hagerty, *The Consequences of Nuclear Proliferation* (Cambridge, MA: MIT Press, 1998).

[45] On the concept of a "limited probe," see Alexander George and Richard Smoke, *Deterrence in American Foreign Policy: Theory and Practice* (New York: Columbia University Press, 1974).

[46] The literature on Kargil, especially from the victorious Indian side, is voluminous. See, e.g., General V. P. Malik, *From Surprise to Victory* (New Delhi: HarperCollins, 2006); Praveen Swami, *The Kargil War* (New Delhi: Leftword, 2000); Amarinder Singh, *A Ridge Too Far: War in the Kargil Heights 1999* (Patiala, India: Motibagh Palace, 2001); Major-General Ashok Krishna and P. R. Chari, ed., *Kargil. The Tables Turned* (New Delhi: Manohar, 2001).

[47] For a partial and obviously partisan discussion, see Pervez Musharraf, *In the Line of Fire* (New York: Simon and Schuster, 2006).

[48] This proposition, to a degree, is confirmed in General Musharraf's memoir; see ibid.

[49] On this subject, see Altaf Gauhar, "Four Wars and One Assumption," *The Nation* (Pakistan), September 5, 1999.

be incorrect. The global community in general, and the United States in particular, took Pakistan to task and made clear that it had to withdraw its troops that had crossed the Line of Control (the de facto international border in the disputed state).

Militarily, though initially caught by surprise, the Indians made a swift recovery and launched a relentless operation designed to force the Pakistanis to withdraw. Facing military defeat and lacking international support the Pakistanis did fall back to the status quo ante by the end of the summer of 1999. Since the Kargil war, despite various bilateral efforts at peacemaking, the two sides have remained at odds. Matters worsened when General Pervez Musharraf, the chief of staff of the Pakistan Army, and the principal architect of Kargil, seized power in October 1999.[50] India's leadership, who had long distrusted military regimes, saw the coup as a particularly disturbing portent.

Diplomatic progress between India and Pakistan has been glacial since Musharraf's coup, despite American pressure on both sides to reach an accommodation regarding Kashmir – especially following the terrorist attacks of September 11, 2001. Nor did India's dramatic exercise in coercive diplomacy in the wake of the December 13, 2001, terrorist attack on its Parliament yield any long-term and tangible benefits despite repeated professions of ending support for terror on the part of General Musharraf.[51] According to Indian and Pakistani accounts, there was an attempt at a peace process from 2004 to 2007. It is also believed that the peace process made considerable headway, with the two sides having agreed on some fundamental principles toward settling a host of long-standing differences. However, it unraveled as a consequence of Musharraf's substantial domestic troubles and the demise of his regime in August 2008.[52]

---

[50] On the October coup, see Sumit Ganguly, "Pakistan's Never-ending Story: Why the October Coup Was No Surprise," *Foreign Affairs* 79:2 (2000): 2–9. Also see Owen Bennett-Jones, *Pakistan: Eye of the Storm* (New Haven, CT: Yale University Press, 2003).

[51] For a detailed discussion, see Ganguly and Hagerty, *Fearful Symmetry*.

[52] Saeed Shah, "Pervez Musharraf Resigns as President of Pakistan," *The Guardian*, August 18, 2008.

Subsequently, on November 26, 2008, a brazen, vicious, and horrific terrorist attack wracked the city of Bombay (Mumbai). Electronic-intelligence intercepts firmly established that the attackers were associated with the Lashkar-e-Taiba, a particularly intransigent terrorist organization based in Pakistan. The attack, which took several days to quell, resulted in extensive material damage and cost the lives of 166 individuals and ten terrorists.[53]

The terrorist attack crippled the limping peace process as Indian decision makers drew it to a close. Subsequently, talks were revived with the new civilian regime of President Asif Ali Zardari but to very little effect. Initially, the two sides had agreed to renew discussions after a multilateral meeting at Sharm-el-Sheikh in Egypt during July 2009. However, the wording of the joint communiqué at this meeting became the subject of intense controversy in India and thereby held up a renewal of discussions.[54] Nevertheless, thanks to the persistence of Prime Minister Manmohan Singh, foreign secretary–level talks did take place in February 2010. Unfortunately, these failed to make much progress.[55] Nevertheless, India's foreign minister, S. M. Krishna, no doubt at the behest of the prime minister, went to Pakistan for discussions with his counterpart Shah Mehmood Qureshi. These talks ended on an acrimonious note leaving the prospects of a future dialogue fraught with uncertainty.[56]

The troubles with Pakistan reflect a fundamental, structural fault that runs across the political landscape of the subcontinent. For the Pakistani politico-military elite, the Kashmir

---

[53] Angel Rabasa, Robert D. Blackwill, Peter Chalk, Kim Cragin, C. Christine Fair, Brian A. Jackson, Brian Michael Jenkins, Seth G. Jones, Nathaniel Sheslak, and Ashley J. Tellis, *The Lessons of Mumbai* (Santa Monica, CA: Rand Corporation, 2009).

[54] See Amitabh Mattoo, "Pakistan Policy: Sharm-el-Sheikh and After," *The Hindu*, September 3, 2009.

[55] Dean Nelson, "India-Pakistan Talks End in Acrimony," *The Telegraph*, February 25, 2010.

[56] Sumit Ganguly, "Get Tough on Pakistan: Its Army Is Fighting against Peace," *Newsweek International*, August 9, 2010.

dispute involves the unfinished business of the partition of the subcontinent in 1947. They remain unreconciled to the status of Kashmir and entertain an irredentist claim on the disputed state.[57] India refuses to countenance any possible territorial compromise as it fears that concessions in Kashmir could have a demonstration effect on other, ethnic secessionist movements.

India and the Northern Colossus

A second shift started in terms of India's relations with the PRC. Confronted with the Soviet collapse and acutely cognizant of the anemic state of Russia – the principal successor state to the Soviet Union – Indian policy makers sought possible ways to engage the PRC. This process of engagement had already started, albeit in a fitful fashion, when the then Indian minister for external affairs, Atal Behari Vajpayee, had visited China in 1977.[58] China's invasion of Vietnam during the very week that Vajpayee was in Beijing had marred the visit. Vajpayee had cut short his visit because of an invidious remark that a Chinese official had made during the visit about "teaching Vietnam a lesson."[59]

The first attempt at a real thaw came in June 1981 when the PRC's foreign minister, Huang Hua, visited India. During this visit he informed his Indian hosts that the PRC was willing to delink progress with India on various fronts despite the persistence of the border dispute and India's unhappiness over China's substantial military assistance to

---

[57] Myron Weiner, "The Macedonian Syndrome: An Historical Model of International Relations and Political Development," *World Politics* 23:4 (1971): 665–83. Also see Ganguly, *Conflict Unending.*

[58] Sumit Ganguly, "The Sino-Indian Border Talks, 1981–1989: A View from New Delhi," *Asian Survey* 29:12 (1989): 1123–35.

[59] Harlan Jencks, "Lessons of a 'Lesson': China-Vietnam, 1979," in *The Lessons of Recent Wars in the Third World*, vol. 1, *Approaches and Case Studies*, ed. Robert E. Harkavy and Stephanie G. Neuman (Lanham, MD: Lexington Books, 1985), ch. 7.

Pakistan.[60] Following his visit some eight rounds of talks were held to address the border dispute. However, these talks, conducted at the level of senior bureaucrats, failed to find a solution. According to a senior Indian official who was closely associated with these talks, both sides agreed to raise the level of the discussions to the ministerial level to seek a possible breakthrough.[61] Accordingly, Rajiv Gandhi visited Beijing in December 1988. It is possible that during his visit to Beijing some discussion ensued about delinking the border dispute from improving the overall tenor of Sino-Indian relations. Finally, during Prime Minister Li Peng's visit to India in December 1991, this principle was formally included in a joint communiqué.[62]

What explained India's reticence to accept the principle of delinking? Two possible explanations can be adduced. One noted scholar argues that the lack of progress on the Sino-Indian border talks between 1982 and 1986 combined with a military confrontation with China in 1987 at Sumdurong Chu led the Rajiv Gandhi regime in India to bring about this policy shift. This explanation, however, is less than compelling.[63] Why would the lack of progress and a military confrontation in a critical area along the border lead the Indian government to adopt a policy of greater flexibility?

A more plausible explanation involves looking at the structural shifts that were taking place in global politics during the late 1980s. With the ascension of Mikhail Gorbachev in Moscow, Soviet policies toward the Third World were undergoing a fundamental shift. Indian policy makers were hardly unaware of these changes. They already had some inkling that the virtually uncritical support that the Soviet Union had

---

[60] John W. Garver, *The Protracted Contest: Sino-Indian Rivalry in the Twentieth Century* (Seattle: University of Washington Press, 2001), 219–20.
[61] Personal interview with a senior Indian diplomat, New Delhi, December 1988.
[62] Garver, *The Protracted Contest*, 221.
[63] Ibid.

provided them since 1971 was now coming to a close.[64] Thus, during 1991, in the wake of the Soviet collapse, it made eminent sense for India to move toward rapprochement with the PRC; now delinking was an attractive option.

Developments in the region also reinforced the incentives stemming from systemic changes. In 1989, a major ethnoreligious insurgency had erupted in the Indian-controlled portion of Jammu and Kashmir. The origins of this insurgency were indigenous.[65] However, in an attempt to exploit an already volatile situation, Pakistan had entered the fray and had dramatically escalated the level of violence in the conflict. During the spring of 1990 India and Pakistan had come to the brink of war.[66] Under these fraught conditions it behooved India to try and improve its relations with its behemoth northern neighbor in order to reduce the possibilities of a two-front conflict.

Not surprisingly, during the 1990s the two sides made significant progress in the realm of a confidence-building measure, most notably with two agreements.[67] The first was signed in 1993 by the Chinese premier, Li Peng, and the Indian prime minister, Narasimha Rao. The second was reached in November 1996 when President Ziang Zemin visited New Delhi. This agreement was particularly significant as one of its clauses stated that, "Neither side shall use its military capability against the other side."[68] According to some observers this amounted to a virtual no-war pact.

[64] Personal interview with an Indian diplomat, Institute of World Affairs, Salisbury, CT, August 1986.

[65] On this subject, see Ganguly, *The Crisis in Kashmir*.

[66] Ganguly and Hagerty, *Fearful Symmetry*.

[67] For a discussion of the significance of these agreements, see Garver, *The Protracted Contest*; also see Rosemary Foot, "Chinese-Indian Relations and the Process of Building Confidence: Implications for the Asia Pacific," *The Pacific Review* 9:1 (1996): 58–76.

[68] "Agreement Between the Government of the People's Republic of China and the Government of the Republic of India on Confidence Building Measures in the Military Field Along the Line of Actual Control in the China-India Border Areas," art. 1.

Relations continued to improve, although progress on the border talks was glacial.[69] Progress on other fronts, however, suffered an important blow when India chose to conduct a set of nuclear tests in May 1998. In the wake of these tests, Prime Minister Vajpayee sent a note to President Clinton in which he alluded to and sought to justify the tests because of a perceived threat from "an overt nuclear weapons state on our borders, a state which committed armed aggression against India in 1962." The letter, which was then leaked to the *New York Times*, infuriated the Chinese leadership, who were already distressed with the Indian nuclear tests. Sino-Indian relations, which had become strained in the immediate aftermath of the tests, worsened considerably.[70]

Despite the tensions that ensued from the tests and the subsequent letter, India managed to repair the damage to the relationship slowly. By March 2000, the two countries had started a new security dialogue and resumed past confidence-building measures.[71] Despite the resumption of this dialogue and an end to public acrimony, there has been pitiably little progress on the border question. Although trade relations have dramatically expanded during the past several years, the two states continue to view each other warily while avoiding significant public disagreements. Apart from the unresolved border issue several differences continue to dog Sino-Indian relations. Among other matters, both states are rapidly emerging as major competitors for global hydrocarbon resources and have competed for access to oil and gas fields from Angola to Kazakhstan.[72] India also remains uneasy about a growing Chinese military presence in Burma/Myanmar and

[69] Sujit Dutta, "Sino Indian Diplomatic Negotiations: A Preliminary Assessment," *Strategic Analysis* 22:12 (March 1999): 1821–34.

[70] On Chinese official reactions to the tests, see Mark W. Frazier, "China-India Relations since Pokhran II: Assessing Sources of Conflict and Cooperation," *AccessAsia Review* 3:2 (2000): 5–36.

[71] Ibid.

[72] Pramit Mitra and Drew Thompson, "China and India: Rivals or Partners?" *Far Eastern Economic Review* (April 2005): 30–3.

China's close ties to the military regime in Pakistan. In an attempt to counter China's increasing influence in Burma/Myanmar, India has abandoned its policy of isolating the military junta there.[73]

In 2009, Sino-Indian relations showed further signs of fraying as the PRC continued to publicly question the status of the northeastern Indian state of Arunachal Pradesh. The Chinese equivocation about the status of the territory came in the wake of its unsuccessful attempt to block an Asian Development Bank loan to India, a part of which would be used to develop hydroelectric resources in the state.[74]

Subsequently, in August 2010, allegations of Chinese military presence in Pakistan-controlled Kashmir caused much concern in India. Subsequently, the PRC's decision not to grant a visa to General B. S. Jaswal, the Northern Command commander of the Indian Army, led India to temporarily halt all military-to-military exchanges with the PRC.[75] These episodes underscore the potential problems that India is likely to encounter as China's economic and military prowess grows apace. Accordingly, it remains to be seen how Indian policy makers forge an appropriate policy that can cope with the changing distribution of power in Asia and beyond.

India and the United States: Bearing the Burdens of the Past

A third and final shift involved relations with the United States. Indo-U.S. relations, for a variety of complex reasons,

[73] Celia W. Dugger, "Indian Aide's Visit Warms Ties with Burmese Junta," *New York Times*, February 16, 2001.

[74] Edward Wong, "China and India Dispute Enclave on Edge of Tibet," *New York Times*, September 4, 2009; for a broader discussion of Sino-Indian tensions, see James Lamont and Amy Kazmin, "Fear of Influence," *Financial Times*, July 13, 2009.

[75] Suman Sharma, "Lt Gen BS Sharma Had Visited China in 2008," *Daily News and Analysis*, August 28, 2010; also see Reuters, "India Cancels All Defence Exchanges with China," *Daily News and Analysis*, August 27, 2010.

had never acquired much ballast, let alone warmth, during the Cold War.[76] India did not have profound cultural ties with the United States, it lacked vital mineral or other natural resources, and it posed no threat to the United States. Additionally, as mentioned earlier, the key architect of its foreign policy, Nehru, had chosen to remain studiously aloof from the United States. His successors had not changed Nehru's policies and, as a consequence of two critical episodes, had come to harbor a deep sense of distrust of the United States. These two episodes – Lyndon Johnson's infamous "ship to mouth" or "short tether" policies during the 1966 food crisis and Richard Nixon's "tilt" policy toward Pakistan during the 1971 Bangladesh crisis – have been described in detail elsewhere and will not be recounted here.[77] Subsequently, India's close relationship with the Soviet Union had done little to endear the country to American policy makers. Consequently, barring some minor interest in India during the Carter administration, in the words of Senator (and previously, Ambassador to India) Daniel Patrick Moynihan, the United States had followed a policy of "benign neglect."

As discussed earlier, in the aftermath of the Soviet invasion of Afghanistan, the United States had come to rely heavily on the military dictatorship of General Zia-ul-Haq in order to militarily render the Soviet occupation very costly. Given the Reagan administration's support for Pakistan and Indira Gandhi's reflexive anti-Americanism, the thaw that came about in 1981 constitutes an important puzzle. Their meeting,

[76] The literature on this subject is voluminous. For a standard diplomatic history, see Dennis Kux, *India and the United States: Estranged Democracies, 1941–1991* (Washington, DC: National Defense University Press, 1992).

[77] On the 1966 crisis, see Sumit Ganguly, "Of Great Hopes and Bitter Disappointments: U.S. Policy toward India during the Johnson Administration," *Asian Affairs* 15:4 (1988–9): 212–19; On Nixon's "tilt" policy, see Christopher Van Hollen, "The Tilt Policy Revisited: Nixon-Kissinger Geopolitics and South Asia," *Asian Survey* 20:4 (1980): 339–61.

which took place on the sidelines of the summit, provided the basis of a very limited rapprochement.[78] Despite minor efforts at the improvement of relations during the two Reagan administrations, the divergent policies of the two states and the lack of other substantial links ensured that there was no breakthrough in Indo-U.S. relations. Matters did not improve substantially under the George H.W. Bush administration for the same reasons.

The relationship showed signs of acquiring some weight during the first Clinton administration. The administration had made domestic and international economic policies key elements of its foreign policy. Accordingly, his first secretary of commerce, Ron Brown, correctly designated India as one of the eight "big emerging markets."[79] Despite this interest in the burgeoning Indian market, the administration's ability to engage India was hobbled because of two other global concerns. First, it was passionately committed to the cause of nonproliferation and thereby sought to "cap, roll back and ultimately eliminate weapons of mass destruction" in South Asia.[80] This policy put India at clear loggerheads with the United States. Second, the administration had adopted a strident, if rather inconsistent, position on promoting human rights globally.[81] This policy had led it to sharply criticize Indian human-rights abuses in suppressing the insurgency at Kashmir and, at least on one occasion, to question the legality and legitimacy of Kashmir's accession to India at the time of partition.[82]

---

[78] On this subject, see Kux, *India and the United States*, 387.

[79] Jeffrey E. Garten, "The Big Emerging Markets," *The Columbia Journal of World Business* 31:2 (Summer 1996): 6–31.

[80] Arthur Rubinoff, "Missed Opportunities and Contradictory Policies: Indo-American Relations in the Clinton-Rao Years," *Pacific Affairs* 69:4 (1996–7): 499–517.

[81] On the abject failure of the administration to live up to its own professed standards, see Samantha Power, *A Problem from Hell: America in the Age of Genocide* (New York: Perennial, 2003).

[82] Robin Raphael, the first U.S. secretary of state for South Asian affairs, in a presumably careless moment made an off-the-cuff remark questioning

Subsequently, thanks to the efforts of individuals in the State Department and Defense Department, the administration adopted a set of policies that appeared to show some partiality toward Pakistan. Among other matters, the administration's criticisms of Pakistan's consistent support to the Kashmiri insurgents proved to be rather anemic and anodyne. In 1995, at the urging of the State Department and key individuals within the Washington foreign-policy community, the administration acceded to the Brown Amendment, which lifted a series of sanctions on Pakistan imposed under the terms of the 1985 Pressler Amendment. The effects of the Brown Amendment, though mostly symbolic, nevertheless had an adverse impact on Indo-U.S. relations. Indian analysts saw this decision as yet another example of the administration's willingness to "equate" Pakistan with India, a subject of considerable irritation in New Delhi. They also commented that the United States was aiding Pakistan despite the latter's headlong pursuit of a nuclear-weapons program through a range of clandestine means.[83]

It was not until the second Clinton term that relations improved. Three factors contributed to paving the pathway to a transformation of Indo-U.S. relations. The first was idiosyncratic and the other two stemmed from pivotal events. In 1994, the administration appointed Frank Wisner, a career diplomat, as the ambassador to New Delhi. Wisner, who had no prior experience in the subcontinent, proved to be an extremely energetic and able ambassador. Despite the setback of the Brown Amendment and the apparent hostility of the assistant secretary of state toward India, he managed through his tireless efforts to improve the tenor of relations with India. Wisner, who had previously worked in the Department of

the robustness of Kashmir's accession to India in 1947 while responding to a query from an Indian correspondent at a briefing held at the National Press Club. See Arthur Rubinoff, "Changing Perceptions of India in the United States Congress," *Asian Affairs: An American Review* 28:1 (2001): 37–60.

[83] Rubinoff, "Missed Opportunities and Contradictory Policies," 516.

Defense as a senior official, was able to capitalize and build upon a nascent Indo-U.S military relationship. Prior to his appointment as ambassador in 1992, the Indian defense minister, Sharad Pawar, then a stalwart in the ruling Congress Party, had visited the United States in an effort to promote Indo-U.S. defense ties. In the wake of his visit, the United States and Indian navies conducted their first-ever military exercise in May 1992. Yet as Strobe Talbott quite candidly notes in his excellent diplomatic memoir, *Engaging India*, the country had really not received serious attention from the Clinton administration despite the best of intentions.[84] A series of other, more pressing, global concerns had kept India as a relatively low-level priority for the administration.

It was the Indian nuclear tests of May 1998 that finally focused the attention of the United States on India and South Asia. The tests represented an affront to and a failure of the Clinton administration's unyielding policy on nuclear proliferation in South Asia. Despite this perceived and important setback, the administration appointed Deputy Secretary of State Talbott to negotiate with India in an effort to bring it back into the nonproliferation gyre. The BJP regime, in turn, appointed its minister for external affairs, Jaswant Singh, a noted Indian politician, to negotiate with Talbott. After fourteen extensive rounds of negotiation, India made few, if any, tangible concessions barring a promise to tighten its export control policies.

In the waning days of his second administration, President Clinton visited India. The visit was a stellar success in terms of improving the climate of bilateral relations despite continuing differences on the nuclear front. Clinton, while continuing to express his dismay about India's nuclear choices, lauded its democratic achievements. The George W. Bush administration, ironically, became the principal beneficiary of the improvements that the Clinton administration managed to

---

[84] See Strobe Talbott, *Engaging India: Diplomacy, Democracy and the Bomb* (Washington, DC: Brookings Institution Press, 2004).

engineer in its final days. Yet it would be incorrect to suggest that the breakthrough that has occurred in Indo-U.S. relations is primarily a Clinton legacy. Admittedly, Clinton's unequivocal position against Pakistan during the Kargil crisis had generated much goodwill in India. His visit, with all the accompanying *bonhomie*, had reinforced those sentiments. However, without serious steps toward the resolution of the nuclear conundrum, progress in Indo-U.S. relations would necessarily stall.

It was the Bush administration's willingness to abandon the traditional views about nonproliferation that enabled it to make a fresh start with India. Even before Bush was elected, Condoleezza Rice, who was a close policy adviser to the presidential candidate, had indicated that if the Republicans assumed office, India would be granted an important status in the American foreign-policy calculus.[85] The reasons for the Bush administration's willingness to alter some of the key guiding principles of American foreign policy in general and toward India in particular are complex and merit some discussion.

The Bush administration's overall shift in foreign-policy orientation has been the subject of much scholarly and journalistic discussion.[86] Suffice it to say that, despite the professed commitment during the presidential campaign to a foreign policy that would eschew extensive international commitments, the administration did a *volte-face* in the wake of the September 11 attacks. It also upended America's long-term commitment to multilateral institutions in order to foster diplomatic solutions to extant international conflicts.[87] It either

---

[85] Condoleeza Rice, "Campaign 2000: Promoting the National Interest," *Foreign Affairs* 79:1 (2000): 45–62.

[86] See, e.g., James Mann, *The Rise of the Vulcans: The Rise of Bush's War Cabinet* (New York: Penguin, 2004); Bob Woodward, *Bush at War* (New York: Simon and Schuster, 2004); for a more scholarly account, see Robert Jervis, "Understanding the Bush Doctrine," *Political Science Quarterly* 118:3 (Fall 2003): 365–88.

[87] See the succinct critique in James Chace, "The Death of American Internationalism," *World Policy Journal* 20:2 (Spring 2003): 1–5.

circumvented them altogether or subverted their procedures to the unbridled pursuit of its own agenda. Obviously, this penchant for unilateral action was nowhere more evident than in the lead-up to the invasion of Iraq.

The administration's interest in India, ironically, represented an important continuity with the policies of the Clinton administration with one key difference. As discussed earlier in this chapter, during the Clinton era relations between India and the United States had been held hostage to the differences regarding the nuclear question. No regime in India had proven willing to dismantle its nuclear-weapons program. The Clinton administration had been intent on returning the nuclear genie to the bottle in South Asia. Consequently, this issue had remained as a major impediment to the improvement of relations.

The Bush administration, which was also committed to nonproliferation, adopted a markedly different stance on the question of nonproliferation than that of its predecessor. The Clinton administration had been focused on strengthening global, legal norms of nonproliferation. The Clinton administration was also, when occasion demanded, as it demonstrated in a crisis with North Korea, willing to resort to war in order to enforce those norms. The new administration adopted a more selective approach and one that placed less reliance on treaties and legal obligations to curb proliferation. More to the point, it made a tacit distinction between states that were allies or potential allies and ones that were overtly hostile toward the United States. Not surprisingly, it adopted an unyielding stance toward Iraq, Iran, and North Korea, the unholy trinity that constituted the "axis of evil."

When it came to dealing with India, the administration pursued a different nonproliferation strategy. India's nuclear weapons, the administration reasoned, did not fundamentally threaten American interests. Furthermore, because the administration and India had some shared misgivings about China's rise, it could make common cause with India. These propositions were rarely spelled out in explicit terms. However, without too much difficulty, one could arrive at these conclusions through a process of inference and attribution.

It needs to be underscored that India was not the passive observer and consequent beneficiary of these shifts in American policy. As argued earlier, India had, for the most part, abandoned its shrill and reflexive anti-Americanism as the Cold War had waned. However, the right-of-center BJP regime, which had come to power in a coalition government in 1999, was prepared to go further in order to foster a better relationship with the United States. One of its more surprising moves was the willingness to endorse the American pursuit of National Missile Defense as early as May 2001. In a cautiously worded statement, Minister for External Affairs Jaswant Singh supported Bush's initiative despite the program's scuttling of the 1972 Anti-Ballistic Missile Treaty.[88]

Subsequently, despite differences regarding questions that dealt with Pakistani involvement with terror in Kashmir and beyond and with India's failure to endorse the United States–led invasion of Iraq, the two sides managed to keep the relationship on track.[89] This was possible because of the mutual recognition of the importance of the bilateral relationship. During the Cold War, India could (and did) routinely pique the United States on a range of bilateral and global issues to the acute detriment of the bilateral relationship.[90] A decade after its end, India had developed sufficient stakes in the realms of economics, strategy, and diplomacy to avoid the temptation to unnecessarily needle the United States. The United States, for its part, had also come to recognize the strategic, economic,

---

[88] Ashley Tellis, "The Evolution of U.S.-Indian Ties: Missile Defense in an Emerging Strategic Relationship," *International Security* 304 (Spring 2006): 113–51.

[89] On the differences over Iraq, see Ramananda Sengupta, "No Troops for Iraq, Even under UN: India," *India Abroad*, September 19, 2003, A23; also see Aziz Haniffa, "US Not Buying India's Argument on Troops to Iraq," *India Abroad*, October 10, 2003, A4.

[90] For a discussion of the difficulties during the Cold War see Sumit Ganguly, "South Asia after the Cold War," *The Washington Quarterly* 15:4 (Autumn 1992): 173–88.

and diplomatic significance of India in the post–Cold War global order.

The most dramatic manifestation of this newly forged relationship came during Prime Minister Manmohan Singh's visit to the United States in July 2005.[91] During this visit, the two sides signed an agreement for cooperation in the realm of civilian nuclear energy that holds the promise of sweeping aside thirty years of American efforts to sanction India for its pursuit of nuclear weapons.[92] This agreement was possible because under the aegis of a set of negotiations, known as the Next Steps in the Strategic Partnership, cooperation in a number of strategic arenas had been pursued with some vigor. These negotiations dealt with four critical and contentious arenas in the relationship: missile defense, civilian nuclear energy, high-technology trade, and civilian space cooperation.[93] The purpose of these discussions was to remove existing legal and institutional obstacles – on both sides – to increased cooperation in these four issue areas.

Crossing the Nuclear Rubicon

Few choices in India's foreign and security policies have elicited as much commentary as the decision to test a set of nuclear weapons in May 1998.[94] India had demonstrated its capability

---

[91] Lauren Etter, "India: Global Partner or Nuclear Threat?" *The Wall Street Journal*, March 4–5, 2006, A7.

[92] Sumit Ganguly and Dinshaw Mistry, "The Case for the U.S.-India Nuclear Agreement," *World Policy Journal* 23:2 (Summer 2006): 11–19.

[93] V. Sudarshan, "Booster Shots," *Outlook* (New Delhi), April 15, 2004, 22–3; also see Ashley Tellis, "Lost Tango in Washington," *The Indian Express*, November 15, 2004.

[94] For a historically detailed but analytically flawed account of the evolution of India's nuclear-weapons program, see George Perkovich, *India's Nuclear Bomb: The Impact on Global Proliferation* (Berkeley: University of California Press, 1999). For an account focused on the early years of the program, see Itty Abraham, *The Making of the Indian Atomic Bomb: Science, Secrecy and the Postcolonial State* (New York: St. Martin's Press, 1998). Also see Ashok Kapur, *Pokhran and Beyond: India's Nuclear Behavior* (New Delhi: Sage Publications, 2002). For the views of Indian scholars, analysts, and former

to manufacture and test a nuclear device as early as May 1974. Widespread international disapprobation and substantial pressures had inhibited future regimes from carrying out any further tests.[95] After the 1974 test, which its policy makers had described as a "peaceful nuclear device," India pursued a policy of nuclear ambiguity. Publicly, it continued to echo much of the earlier Nehruvian rhetoric about its staunch commitment to rid the world of nuclear weapons through a process of global nuclear disarmament. At the same time, it continued inexorably to pursue a subterranean nuclear-weapons program. In the 1970s, the principal perceived threat emanated from the PRC.[96] The program acquired greater momentum during the next decade as Pakistan accelerated its own clandestine program and obtained substantial assistance from the PRC, which significantly boosted its pursuit of nuclear weapons and ballistic missiles.[97] Faced with the growth of Pakistani capabilities, in 1984, Prime Minister Rajiv Gandhi, shortly after assuming office, gave his assent to the Integrated Guided Missile Development Program. Under the aegis of this program, the Defense Research and Development Organization was tasked to produce a spectrum of short-, medium-, and long-range ballistic missiles.[98]

policy makers, see Amitabh Mattoo, ed., *India's Nuclear Deterrent: Pokhran II and Beyond* (New Delhi: Har Anand, 1999) and Jasjit Singh, ed., *Nuclear India* (New Delhi: South Asia Books, 1998). For a formulation that seeks to explain India's acquisition of nuclear weapons as a consequence of external security threats, see Sumit Ganguly, "India's Pathway to Pokhran II: The Sources and Prospects of India's Nuclear Weapons Program," *International Security* 23:4 (1999): 148–77. For a comprehensive account of the future of the Indian nuclear-weapons program see Ashley Tellis, *India's Emerging Nuclear Posture: Between Recessed Deterrent and Ready Arsenal* (Santa Monica, CA: Rand Corporation, 2001).

[95] Sumit Ganguly, "Why India Joined the Nuclear Club," *Bulletin of the Atomic Scientists* 39:4 (1982): 30–33.

[96] Ganguly, "India's Pathway to Pokhran II."

[97] Garver, *The Protracted Contest*; also see Rodney W. Jones, *Tracking Nuclear Proliferation: A Guide in Maps and Charts* (Washington, DC: Carnegie Endowment for International Peace, 1998).

[98] Chris Smith, *India's Ad Hoc Arsenal: Direction or Drift in Defense Policy* (Oxford: Oxford University Press, 1994).

Throughout the 1980s and beyond, the Indian nuclear-weapons and ballistic-missile programs proceeded apace.[99] The United States, for its part, continued to verbally and materially oppose the Indian efforts thereby contributing to an important source of tension in the bilateral relationship. In the 1990s, Indian diplomats watched helplessly as the United States, through a deft amalgam of pressure, cajolery, and skill, managed to obtain an unconditional and indefinite extension of the Nuclear Nonproliferation Treaty (NPT). India, along with Israel and Pakistan, remained the only holdout states. The successful extension of the NPT left India isolated to a very large extent in the global order. Yet the NPT alone would not hobble India's efforts to maintain its nuclear option.

In 1992, India had cosponsored a resolution with the United States to bring about a Comprehensive Test Ban Treaty (CTBT). However, as the CTBT proceeded apace in Geneva at the Conference on Disarmament, India's negotiators developed a number of reservations. Among other matters, they argued that the original intent of the CTBT, which had been to ban all forms of nuclear testing, would not be accomplished in the draft that was emerging. They contended that the draft treaty contained far too many loopholes.

In the late 1990s, despite Indian reservations about its final form and various attempts to prevent it from being reported to the General Assembly from the Conference on Disarmament, the United States managed to move the draft to the UN General Assembly for a vote. In the UN General Assembly, it successfully enlisted the support of the vast majority of the member states to support a CTBT. India, which had been the original proponent of this treaty, now stood in opposition to it.[100]

Once the treaty passed the UN General Assembly, the Indian political establishment had reason to fret. According

---

[99] Raju G. C. Thomas, "India's Nuclear and Space Programs," *World Politics* 38:2 (January 1986): 315–42.

[100] Dinshaw Mistry, "The Unrealized Promise of International Institutions: The Test Ban Treaty and India's Nuclear Breakout," *Security Studies* 12:4 (Summer 2003): 116–51.

to a critical clause in the CTBT, some forty-four states with ongoing nuclear-power and research programs were required to ratify it before September 1998 in order to ensure its entry into force. According to India's calculations, this was obviously directed at holdout states such as Pakistan and India. Not surprisingly, the Indian leadership realized that the window of opportunity to test its existing stockpile of nuclear weapons was rapidly closing. Once the BJP-led coalition government came to power, it lost little time in making preparations for carrying out a series of nuclear tests. A small group of trusted individuals close to Prime Minister Vajpayee made the decision to carry out a series of tests during the early days of the new regime.[101] Once this political decision was made, the Indian nuclear establishment moved with considerable dispatch, skill, and dexterity to make the preparations for the tests without detection.[102]

The Indian decision to cross the nuclear Rubicon was met with considerable international disapprobation. The United States, in particular, led the charge to diplomatically isolate India. This effort, however, proved to be largely unsuccessful.[103] Over time, the bulk of the sanctions that had been imposed on India, barring those dealing with critical dual-use technologies, were steadily removed.

Belated Recognition: India and Southeast Asia

Attempts to shift India's foreign policy toward Southeast Asia also occurred as the 1970s drew to a close. However, it is a little-known fact that the Indian leadership had spurned the overtures of the founders of the Association of Southeast Asian Nations

---

[101] Personal interview with senior, retired Indian policy maker, New Delhi, August 2006.

[102] For a detailed discussion, see Raj Chengappa, *Weapons of Peace: The Secret Story of India's Quest to be a Nuclear Power* (New Delhi: HarperCollins, 2000).

[103] Much of this effort is discussed at considerable length in Talbott, *Engaging India*.

(ASEAN) when it was being formed. India's leaders had felt that the organization, composed exclusively of states that had close ties to the United States, was simply another anti-Communist and anti-Soviet bastion in Asia, and that India could ill-afford to become a member of any such organization. Such membership would have inevitably compromised its nonaligned credentials. The irony of India's refusal to join this nascent organization should not be overlooked. Prior to and even after its independence, India had been a staunch advocate of "Asian solidarity," and a number of its leaders, including Nehru, had visualized an Asia that would make common cause on a range of international questions once freed from the colonial yoke.[104]

India finally changed its policy in 1979 when it sought observer status in ASEAN. Unfortunately, India's recognition of the Vietnamese-installed government in Cambodia made the ASEAN states reluctant to accept India as a full-dialogue partner. After some careful negotiations, India was invited to join the dialogue with ASEAN in 1980. However, owing to the exigencies of Indian domestic politics, India was unable to dispatch Minister for External Affairs Narasimha Rao to the ministerial meeting in Kuala Lumpur. Consequently, India's admission into this body got deferred. It was not until after Narasimha Rao became prime minister, following the deaths of both Indira and Rajiv Gandhi, that India became a "sectoral partner" of ASEAN.[105] Two years later, in December 1995, India was made a full-dialogue partner of ASEAN at the Bangkok ASEAN Summit. The next year, India was made a member of the ASEAN Regional Forum (ARF). Since India's entry into ARF it has steadily increased its presence in Southeast Asia and has sought to foster important commercial and military ties with a range of states in the region extending from Vietnam to Singapore.

---

[104] See the careful discussion in T. A. Keenleyside, "Nationalist Indian Attitudes towards Asia: A Troublesome Legacy for Post-Independence Indian Foreign Policy," *Pacific Affairs* 55:2 (1982): 210–30.

[105] Ramesh Thakur, *The Politics and Economics of India's Foreign Policy* (London: C. Hurst and Company, 1994), 237–8.

The commercial and trade relationships that India is attempting to foster with the fast-growing economies of the region do not require much comment. However, it is important to underscore that India's armed forces are now an increasing presence in the region. Indian naval vessels have made a series of port visits to Vietnam, a country with which India has long enjoyed good relations. India has made a concerted effort to improve relations with Malaysia, a country that has long had good relations with China, but that is now interested in hedging its bets.[106] The Singaporean Air Force has signed an agreement with the Indian Air Force to use Indian air bases for conducting practice bombing runs, and India has agreed to refurbish Malaysian Air Force aircraft. In the wake of the September 11 attacks on the United States, the Indian Navy also conducted extensive joint patrolling of the Straits of Malacca with the U.S. Seventh Fleet. More recently, India participated in an ad hoc coalition, involving the United States, Japan, and Australia, to provide relief to the tsunami-affected regions of the Indian Ocean littoral states in January 2005.[107] India's growing military presence in the region is part of a carefully orchestrated strategy to counter the PRC's attempts to extend its influence in the region.[108] Such a strategy, though belated, is in keeping with India's perception of itself as an emerging Asian power with significant commercial, diplomatic, and strategic interests in Southeast Asia.[109] Despite various constraints – financial and organizational – India will play an increasingly prominent role in the Indian Ocean littoral.[110]

[106] M. G. G. Pillai, "Archipelago of Dreams," *Outlook* (New Delhi), February 12, 2001.

[107] Gurpreet Khurana, "Cooperation among Maritime Security Forces: Imperatives for India and Southeast Asia," *Strategic Analysis* 29:2 (2005): 295–317.

[108] James F. Hoge Jr., "A Global Power Shift in the Making," *Foreign Affairs* (July/August 2004): 2–7.

[109] Christopher Griffin, "Containment with Chinese Characteristics:Beijing Hedges against the Rise of India," *Asian Outlook* 3 (September 2006), http://www.aei.org/outlook/24873 (accessed January 15, 2011).

[110] Donald L. Berlin, "India in the Indian Ocean," *Naval War College Review* 59:2 (Spring 2006): 58–89.

Conclusions and Policy Recommendations

The transformation that has taken place in India's foreign policy is nothing short of revolutionary. As we have sought to sketch out in this chapter, an interaction of structure and agency best explains this dramatic shift. The Cold War's end made it exceedingly difficult for India to continue with its policies of nonalignment and Third World solidarity. Yet structure alone cannot fully explain the changes that came about. Unless key individuals at critical junctures had chosen to undertake different pathways and seize opportune moments, India would have faced the distinct possibility of marginalization in the emergent global order. Fortunately, a set of largely felicitous and bold choices enabled the country to avoid such a fate. The task ahead is to ensure that it does not lapse into backsliding as it confronts new challenges.

To do so will require India's policy makers to monitor the changed and evolving structure of the global order carefully and fashion policies and strategies that best serve India's national interests. To that end, they will have to forge a national consensus regarding key goals and objectives for India's foreign and security policies. During the Cold War, in a rough and ready fashion, the doctrine of nonalignment served this purpose. In the new global order, India cannot content itself with allusions to "enlightened self-interest" and the quest for "strategic autonomy"[111] and a preference for a multipolar global order. Instead, it needs to devise a new set of overarching moral and intellectual principles that might enable it to help shape the emergent global order. To that end its strategic elites need to begin a discussion of the principles that might undergird India's foreign policy.[112]

It is beyond the scope of this chapter to predict and discuss the potential challenges that India's foreign-policy decision

---

[111] Guillem Monsonis, "India's Strategic Autonomy and Rapprochment with the U.S.," *Strategic Analysis* 34:4 (July 2010): 611–24.

[112] Press Trust of India, "India, China and Russia for Multi-Polar World," *Financial Express*, February 15, 2007.

makers will face in the years ahead. However, it is possible to sketch some of the likely issues they will confront. First, India must evolve a long-term strategy to deal with its nettlesome neighbor, Pakistan. Second, it will have to maintain its dual-track policy toward China and avoid the propensity to either demonize China or overlook the serious threats that certain forms of Chinese behavior may pose for India's long-term security interests. Third, India will have to place its relations with the United States on a stable and secure footing. It is relatively easy to sketch out these possible challenges. It is a far more difficult task to provide clear-cut guidance regarding how these ends may be accomplished.

Nevertheless, some straightforward propositions can be spelled out. India has to accept that Pakistan will remain a recalcitrant and difficult neighbor for the foreseeable future. Pakistan's unyielding commitment to wrest Kashmir from India will not dissipate easily.[113] Thanks to critical choices on the part of civilian and military elites, the issue has become deeply embedded in Pakistan's political culture.[114] At best, India should attempt to restore law and order within its portion of Kashmir, thereby reducing Pakistan's ability to engage in mischief making in this long-troubled region.[115] This will entail pursuing sustained political negotiations with the Kashmiri populace and continuing efforts to suppress the Pakistan-backed insurgents militarily. Eventually, although stable peace with Pakistan may be impossible, repeated crises in Indo-Pakistani relations can also be avoided if a modicum of law and order prevail in Kashmir.

Indian policy toward the PRC has tended to oscillate from warm expressions of friendship and amity to dire fears

---

[113] Sumit Ganguly, "General Kayani: A Musharraf in the Making," *Times of India Crest*, March 20, 2010.

[114] On this subject, see Husain Haqqani, *Pakistan: Between Mosque and Military* (Washington, DC: Carnegie Endowment for International Peace, 2005). Also see Bennett-Jones, *Pakistan: Eye of the Storm*.

[115] On this subject, see Sumit Ganguly, "The Kashmir Conundrum," *Foreign Affairs* 85:4 (2006): 45–57.

of imminent and serious conflict. Indian policy makers need to develop a more coherent and realistic policy toward the PRC that avoids such extraordinary shifts. They will have to come to terms with the fact that the PRC and India will remain caught in a competitive relationship. Both states aspire to regional and great-power status. Unfortunately for India, the PRC, based upon virtually every reliable indicator of "hard power," is ahead.[116] Though the relationship is likely to remain competitive, careful diplomacy combined with a degree of military preparedness can prevent the outbreak of a conflict with the PRC. Simultaneously, India's leaders must also eschew any false expectation that increased trade, commerce, and other contacts will necessarily transform this competitive relationship into one that is more cordial and amicable.

The final challenge before India's foreign-policy makers remains the management of the increasingly cordial relationship with the United States. Indo-U.S. relations today, unlike during the Cold War, have acquired a certain ballast and substance. Nevertheless, given the asymmetry in power and concomitant global reach, not to mention a long history of discord and contention, differences are likely to persist in the relationship. The test of India's new and dexterous diplomacy will lie in its ability to contain the differences and build upon the possible arenas of cooperation.[117] More to the point, Indian diplomacy, especially when dealing with the United States, will need to become less reactive. Instead, India's policy makers will have to seek out new avenues of possible cooperation with the United States and pursue them to the mutual benefit of both states.

---

[116] On the distinction between "soft" and "hard" power, see Joseph S. Nye, *Soft Power: The Means to Success in World Politics* (New York: Public Affairs Press, 2004).

[117] For a discussion of the structural forces and political choices that have led the recent transformation of the relationship, see C. Raja Mohan, *Impossible Allies: Nuclear India, United States and the Global Order* (New Delhi: India Research Press, 2006).

In addition to dealing with these critical relationships, India will also need to revamp its foreign-policy-making apparatus in order to cope with the demands of an increasingly complex global order. As a number of astute observers have cogently argued, India, at the outset, needs to expand the size of its foreign service. In 2007, the country had 119 embassies and 49 consulates with a mere six-hundred-odd diplomats.[118] A country that aspires to major power status can ill-afford to have such anemic global representation.

Apart from expanding the size of its foreign service, India also needs to undertake some internal reforms to bolster the capabilities of its foreign-policy-making apparatus. For too long it has relied on able generalists who are expected to acquire expertise in particular areas in their assigned positions. This model is anachronistic and is fundamentally unsuited to meet the demands of a global order that requires specific functional and area expertise. To boost India's ability to conduct complex negotiations in issue areas ranging from arms control to global trade, the foreign service would be wise to develop a cadre of officers who have specialized and competence training in key functional areas.[119]

Finally, the Ministry of External Affairs could also benefit from some organizational reform. A former minister of state for external affairs, Shashi Tharoor, has cogently argued that particular divisions of the ministry have no routine mechanisms in place for policy coordination and formulation. To end such compartmentalization, he had sought to develop a mechanism that might break down such barriers and improve policy coordination through the revitalization of the policy-planning staff within the ministry.[120] Whether such

---

[118] Kishan S. Rana, *Asian Diplomacy: The Foreign Ministries of China, India, Japan, Singapore and Thailand* (Malta and Geneva, Switzerland: DiploFoundation, 2007).

[119] Sumit Ganguly, "Inept Babus Hobble Our Great Power Ambitions," *The Times of India*, December 20, 2009.

[120] Nitin Pai, "The Capacity to Engage," *Pragati: The Indian National Interest Review* 33 (December 2009): 7–12.

much-needed institutional and organizational changes occur in a timely fashion remains an open question. India's past experiences with institutional reform and change do not suggest that they will take place with any dispatch in the absence of a catalytic crisis that would induce a need for sweeping and swift reforms.

3

India's Economic Transformation

How did India make the transition from an economic laggard to one of the most rapidly growing economies in the world? Its sluggish economic development had once been pejoratively described as the "Hindu rate of growth."[1] Industrial modernization and the so-called green revolution could muster a mere 3.4 percent average annual rate of growth between 1956 and 1974, at a time when many Asian economies were booming. But between 1975 and 1990, the country's economic growth accelerated at a rate higher than 5 percent and then increased to more than 6 percent after 1992. Subsequently, the Indian economy grew at 8.8 percent between 2003 and 2007, and thereby transformed itself into one of the fastest-growing economies in the world along with China. The World Bank–International Monetary Fund (IMF) Annual Meeting in Singapore in 2006 was dedicated to the rise of China and India. In the aftermath of the global financial crisis,

---

[1]   The term *Hindu rate of growth*, first used by the Indian economist Raj Krishna, depicted a condition of slow growth in India. See Montek S. Ahluwalia, "Economic Reform for the 1990s," *First Raj Krishna Memorial Lecture* (Jaipur: Department of Economics–University of Rajasthan, 1995), 1, available at http://planningcommission.nic.in/aboutus/speech/spemsa/msa033.pdf (accessed August 20, 2009). This term was used in a secular sense and pointed to traditional Indian social characteristics that were thought to be an impediment to growth.

India continued to grow more rapidly (6.7% during 2008–9) than all the major Asian economies, except China.[2] To address these questions, it is necessary to trace how India embarked upon this growth path. Its policy makers gradually deregulated private-sector investment after 1975.[3] Deregulation from the mid-1970s needs to be understood in the context of a political and economic environment that had produced one of the most highly regulated economies in the world. The phenomenon of industrial deregulation was consolidated in the 1980s. That period was important because it laid the ideational and political foundations for the tectonic policy shifts of 1991. Substantial political opposition to trade liberalization existed during the 1980s, even though the lessons learned from success stories in East Asia had

[2] The Indian economy grew more rapidly in 2008–9 than the economies of countries such as South Korea, Malaysia, Taiwan, Indonesia, Philippines, Vietnam, Russia, and South Africa. China was the one major country whose economy grew more rapidly than India's. Comparative data are from two databases, The World Development Indicators and The World Bank, and the database of the Economist Intelligence Unit, accessed through the National University of Singapore library Web site. For the GDP growth at factor cost in India, see Government of India, *Economic Survey 2008–09* (New Delhi: Ministry of Finance, 2009), 2.

[3] For three important accounts that see 1975 as the year of change, see Baldev R. Nayar, "When Did the 'Hindu' Rate of Growth End?" *Economic and Political Weekly* 41:19 (May 13, 2006): 1885–90; Jessica S. Wallach, "Structural Breaks in Indian Macroeconomic Data," *Economic and Political Weekly* 38:41 (October 11, 2003): 4312–15; Arvind Panagariya, *India: The Emerging Giant* (New Delhi and New York: Oxford University Press, 2008), 80–1. Two other accounts that suggest that the probusiness attitude of the government during the 1980s was responsible for the growth turnaround include Dani Rodrik and Arvind Subramanian, "From 'Hindu Growth' to Productivity Surge: The Mystery of the Indian Growth Transition," *The IMF Working Paper* 04:77 (Washington, DC: International Monetary Fund, 2004): 3–39; Atul Kohli, "The Politics of Economic Growth in India, 1980–2005: Part 1," *Economic and Political Weekly* 41:13 (April 1, 2006): 1251–9. We take the view that policy changes favoring Indian business after 1975 mark a shift in the policy direction.

made a tangible impact on policy makers. It was only after the balance-of-payments crisis in 1991 that substantial economic deregulation favoring the private sector and international trade took place.[4]

India's story of economic development defies the logic of development in many Asian economies that were characterized as hard authoritarian states. Authoritarian "developmental states" in Asia disciplined industrialists, redistributed land, and promoted literacy and public health, which were the prerequisites for competitiveness and economic growth.[5] Farmers, industrialists, and bureaucrats and professionals in India could use their ability to organize themselves effectively in order to oppose trade liberalization and stall the empowerment of the poor and lower-caste groups.[6] How did a state, which became increasingly beholden to business groups, the poor, and lower-caste groups, attend to the problem of promoting competitiveness and human development? What challenges confront the sustenance of economic growth and social development in India?

[4] Jagdish Bhagwati, *India in Transition* (Oxford: Clarendon Press, 1993), 39–69; Vijay Joshi and I. M. D. Little, *India: Macroeconomics and Political Economy* (New Delhi: Oxford University Press, 1994), 180–91; Panagariya, *India: The Emerging Giant*, 95–109; Rahul Mukherji, "Political Economy of Reforms," in *The Oxford Companion to Politics in India*, ed. Niraja G. Jayal and Pratap B. Mehta (New Delhi: Oxford University Press, 2010), 483–98.

[5] Robert Wade, *Governing the Market* (Princeton, NJ: Princeton University Press, 1990); Stephan Haggard, *Pathways from the Periphery* (Ithaca, NY: Cornell University Press, 1988); Peter Evans, *Embedded Autonomy* (Princeton, NJ: Princeton University Press, 1995); Alice Amsden, *Asia's Next Giant* (Oxford: Oxford University Press, 1989).

[6] On the political economy of interest groups favoring the status quo, see Pranab Bardhan, *The Political Economy of Development in India* (Oxford: Basil Blackwell, 1984), 40–59. On why the Indian state enjoyed less autonomy to engineer economic change in the 1980s than in the 1960s, when Prime Minister Nehru was at the helm, see Sudipta Kaviraj, "A Critique of the Passive Revolution," in *State and Politics in India*, ed. Partha Chatterjee (New Delhi: Oxford University Press, 1997), 45–87; Ronald J. Herring, "Embedded Particularism: India's Failed Developmental State," in *The Developmental State*, ed. Meredith Woo-Cummings (Ithaca, NY: Cornell University Press, 1999), 306–34.

This chapter is divided into three sections. The first describes India's economic development between 1947 and 1974. It spells out the process by which the government came to control substantial parts of the country's industry. It tells the story of how the neglect of Indian agriculture was replaced by an emphasis on food security and tells of the country's experiments with the closed economy, which generated neither substantial economic growth nor welfare for its citizenry. The second section analyzes the period from 1975 until 1990. This was a time when India promoted its private enterprises in the context of a closed economy. Its economic growth accelerated, the agricultural sector grew rapidly, and greater attention was paid to the concerns of human development. The final section from 1991 until the present, describes the paradox of the shift to rapid economic growth and globalization in the country, accompanied by rather sluggish progress in the well-being of its citizenry. Politics within a plural democratic polity may be gradually engendering a welfare state, but its trajectory will depend almost entirely on the sustainability of high growth.[7]

The Legacy of Controls in a Self-Reliant Economy: 1947–1974

India's "mixed economy"[8] was born in the immediate aftermath of an anticolonial struggle. The powerful economic development paradigm of import-substituting industrialization justified opposition to a regime of trade-led development. It was believed that infant industries, especially in high-technology

---

[7]   On the relationship between economic growth and welfare expenditure in India, see Baldev R. Nayar, *The Myth of the Shrinking State* (New Delhi: Oxford University Press, 2009), 70–107.

[8]   *Mixed economy* is a term used to connote an economy in which neither the government-owned sectors nor the private sector dominate economic activity. See, e.g., Baldev R. Nayar, *India's Mixed Economy* (Bombay: Popular Prakashan, 1989).

areas, required substantial state-supported finance and protection from international trade until they matured into competitive entities. Moreover, trade was not viewed as an engine of growth.[9] This section provides the political and economic context within which the liberalization measures after 1975 need to be understood.

The contest between the radicals and the moderates within the ruling Congress Party regarding the optimal extent of state intervention after independence produced a compromise that increased the state's commanding position in the 1950s.[10] The powerful Deputy Prime Minister Vallabhbhai Patel (1947–50), until his untimely death in 1950, was opposed to Jawaharlal Nehru's inclination to favor greater state intervention.[11] Nehru was a social democrat who believed that liberal political and economic institutions could deliver economic growth with redistribution. The 1950s witnessed greater state control over industrial activity and the birth of the industrial licensing system, which made it necessary for companies to seek the permission of the government before initiating business in permitted areas.[12] Despite these controls, Nehru's liberal instincts secured a greater role for domestic and foreign corporations than was the case after 1969.

---

[9] On the impact of the import-substituting industrialization paradigm on India and the developing world, see Jagdish Bhagwati and Padma Desai, *India: Planning for Industrialization* (London: Oxford University Press, 1970); Bhagwati, *India in Transition*, 5–11; Anne O. Krueger, *Political Economy of Policy Reform in Developing Countries* (Cambridge, MA: MIT Press, 1995), 37–51.

[10] On how the debate between the economic radicals and liberals was being resolved in favor of the latter during the early years, see Francine R. Frankel, *India's Political Economy: 1947–2004* (New Delhi: Oxford University Press, 2005), 70–7; Medha Kudaisya, *The Life and Times of G. D. Birla* (New Delhi: Oxford University Press, 2003), 305–16; Vivek Chibber, *Locked in Place* (Princeton, NJ: Princeton University Press, 2003), 126–57.

[11] Kudaisya, *The Life and Times of G. D. Birla*, 278–91.

[12] See Frankel, *India's Political Economy*, 70–7; Kudaisya, *The Life and Times of G. D. Birla*, 305–16; Chibber, *Locked in Place*, 126–57.

He was impressed with Soviet economic planning based on rapid capital-intensive industrialization. Accordingly, he promoted a powerful and technocratic Planning Commission and the greater involvement of the state in economic activity aimed at achieving this goal.[13] Capital-intensive industrialization was a constraint on the resources available for agricultural development during the Second Five-Year Plan (1956–61). The total plan outlay in regard to agriculture was substantially reduced during this period.[14] The planners were optimistic that land reforms and cooperative farming, based on small landowners voluntarily participating in the collective management of farms, would spur agricultural growth. State-level Congress Party leaders and the Ministry of Agriculture unsuccessfully opposed the dearth of investment in agriculture.[15] The scarcity of funds needed to finance essential imports produced a foreign-exchange crisis in 1957, despite the neglect of agriculture.

India was faced with political and economic uncertainties after Nehru's death in 1964. The country was living on subsidized wheat shipments from the United States under the U.S. Public Law 480 Program. The United States was skeptical about the merits of India's planning, which was

[13] On the rise of the Planning Commission and industrial regulation, see A. H. Hanson, *The Process of Planning* (London: Oxford University Press, 1966), 122–45; Frankel, *India's Political Economy*, 113–30. For an account on how the Planning Commission was contested but unsuccessfully challenged in the 1950s, see Medha Kudaisya, "'A Mighty Adventure': Institutionalizing the Idea of Planning in Post-colonial India," *Modern Asian Studies* 43:4 (2009): 939–78. Nehru saw a role for the private sector, despite his emphasis on the government. See P. N. Dhar, *The Evolution of Economic Policy in India* (New Delhi: Oxford University Press, 2003), 230–3; Kudaisya, *The Life and Times of G. D. Birla*, 316–21, 331–6.

[14] Frankel, *India's Political Economy*, 131.

[15] On the declining emphasis on Indian agriculture after the second Five-Year Plan see ibid., 131–200; Ashutosh Varshney, *Democracy, Development and the Countryside* (Cambridge: Cambridge University Press, 1998), 28–47.

bedeviled with the problems of implementation and resource mobilization.[16]

Following Nehru's death, his successor Lal Bahadur Shastri (1964–6) initiated significant changes in India's economic policy. He inherited the foreign-exchange problem and had to deal with a war with Pakistan in 1965. The country was also faced with declining food-grain production and inflation. Shastri responded differently from Nehru. First, agriculture was given priority.[17] Second, the power of the Planning Commission, which had favored capital-intensive industrialization over agricultural development, was curbed.[18] Third, decisions were taken to align India's economic policy with the critical report of The World Bank's Bell Commission in 1965 because the infusion of developmental assistance was deemed necessary for India's economic growth.[19] Consequently, the government decided to devalue the rupee, liberalize imports, and increase the role of private and foreign investment.[20]

---

[16] On the United States' aid weariness after 1963, see Bruce Muirhead, "Differing Perspectives: The World Bank and the 1963 Aid India Negotiations," *India Review* 4:1 (January 2005): 1–22; Medha M. Kudaisya, "Reforms by Stealth," *South Asia* 25:2 (August 2002): 216–20; Rahul Mukherji, "India's Foreign Economic Policies," in *India's Foreign Policy: Retrospect and Prospect*, ed. Sumit Ganguly (New Delhi: Oxford University Press, 2009), 301–5.

[17] Varshney, *Democracy, Development and the Countryside*, 49–80; Frankel, *India's Political Economy*, 248–67.

[18] On the rise of the PMO at this time see Frankel, *India's Political Economy*, 251–2.

[19] Bernard Bell of The World Bank was given the task of writing a critical report that could be used to pressure policy change in India in return for financial resources. On the critical Report of the Bell Commission, see David B. H. Denoon, *Devaluation under Pressure* (Cambridge, MA: MIT Press, 1986), 72–5; John P. Lewis, *India's Political Economy* (New Delhi: Oxford University Press, 1997), 138; Benjamin B. King, *Transcript of Interview with Robert W. Oliver* (Washington, DC: The World Bank Oral History Program Archives, July 24–25, 1986), 16–28. Benjamin King authored some parts of the report.

[20] David B. H. Denoon, "Cycles in Indian Economic Liberalization, 1966–1996," *Comparative Politics* 31:1 (October 1998): 49–50.

Indira Gandhi (1966–77, 1980–4), Nehru's daughter, succeeded Shastri in January 1966 after his unexpected death. Faced with external pressures from multilateral donors due to the balance-of-payments problems and a stagnant economy, she was compelled to make substantial changes in the country's economic policy. To that end, she undertook a major devaluation of the rupee. Her decision to devalue the rupee met with widespread opposition in the Indian Parliament. The majority of economists and industrialists at the time opined that devaluation and trade promotion would not serve India well. In fact, it was widely believed that devaluation and trade liberalization were the results of foreign pressure rather than the product of an internally generated consensus in the matter.[21]

The government had learned the lesson of neglecting agriculture; doing so had made it dependent on shipments of food grains from the United States. It pursued a policy of promoting agriculture from the mid-1960s. Two hundred metric tons of high-yielding variety seeds taken from a Mexican strain were successfully cultivated under Indian conditions. The technological and financial assistance from the United States, which led to the doubling of India's wheat output between 1965 and 1970, contributed to the country's green revolution. The green revolution largely benefited farmers with holdings greater than 2.5 acres of land. It made a significant impact on India's food security and contributed toward alleviating poverty in the country.[22] It should be noted that

---

[21] On the opposition to devaluation, see Rahul Mukherji, "India's Aborted Liberalization – 1966," *Pacific Affairs* 73:3 (Fall 2000): 382–9.

[22] On the green revolution, see Francine R. Frankel, *India's Green Revolution: Economic Gains and Political Costs* (Princeton, NJ: Princeton University Press, 1971); Lloyd I. Rudolph and Susanne H. Rudolph, *In Pursuit of Lakshmi: The Political Economy of the Indian State* (Chicago: University of Chicago Press, 1987), 312–92; Varshney, *Democracy, Development and the Countryside*, 50–78. On the impact of the green revolution on poverty, see Manoj Panda, "Agriculture and Poverty Reduction," in *Oxford Handbook of Agriculture*, ed. Shovan Ray (New Delhi: Oxford University Press, 2007), 116–17. The states that benefited the most from the

India agreed to take American advice on agriculture but not in the area of industrial policy.[23]

In the aftermath of the rupee devaluation and the domestic political fallout, Indira Gandhi undertook another sharp shift in economic policy making. Accordingly, India entered the most intensely state-driven and autarkic phase of its industrialization between 1969 and 1974. First, there was a mismatch between Indian and American expectations. The Indian establishment was of the view that it had done its best, despite serious internal opposition, to satisfy the Aid India Consortium and The World Bank.[24] The U.S. establishment considered this response rather inadequate. Furthermore, given Indira Gandhi's critical views about the U.S. intervention in Vietnam, President Lyndon Johnson placed India's food-grain shipments on a short tether, with presidential consent required for every shipment of food grain that was sent out.[25] Second, Indira Gandhi turned to the Left for political reasons. She felt insecure in the company of the senior right-wing political leadership within the Congress Party. Congress leaders such as Kumarasami Kamraj and Morarji Desai had treated her as dispensable once the leadership issue was sorted out. To make her position secure, she aligned herself with the Communist Party of India and mobilized the Congress Forum for Socialist Action. In 1969 she distanced herself from the old guard of the Congress Party by creating a separate party, the Congress (R), which included the younger and left-leaning members of the Congress Party.[26]

---

green revolution also had the lowest number of people living below the poverty line.

[23] Lewis, *India's Political Economy*, 135.

[24] On the compulsions of the Indian side, see Mukherji, "India's Aborted Liberalization – 1966," 381–9.

[25] For the U.S. side of the story, see James Warner Bjorkman, "Public Law 480 and Policies of Self-Help and Short-Tether," in *The Regional Imperative*, ed. Lloyd I. Rudolph and Susanne H. Rudolph (Atlantic Highlands, NJ: Humanities Press, 1980), 232–3.

[26] Congress (R) stood for Congress (Reform). For an account of the politics that led to the creation of Congress (R), see Vernon Hewitt,

Domestic political opposition to devaluation and liberalization, and Prime Minister Gandhi's alliance with the Left ensured that the state curbed all private-sector activities to the greatest extent possible between 1969 and 1974. First, the Monopolies and Restrictive Trade Practices Act (MRTP, 1969) placed stringent regulations on any private company worth more than 200 million rupees ($4.3 million). Second, the Foreign Exchange Regulation Act (FERA, 1974) restricted the maximum equity participation in an Indian firm to 40 percent. Limitation of foreign-equity participation after the imposition of FERA reduced the powers of foreign companies in the governance of their Indian subsidiaries. This became a significant disincentive for foreign investors. Third, large parts of the Indian economy, which included sectors such as steel, copper, banking, insurance, and the wheat trade, were nationalized.[27]

State control and autarkic industrialization were supposed to contribute to poverty alleviation and human development. However, these expectations were not met. The Indian economy grew at a dismal average annual rate of 3.4 percent between 1956 and 1974; the poverty ratio, or the total number of people below the poverty line, did not register a decline between 1951 and 1974. The poverty line in these calculations was defined as 57 rupees ($7.36) per capita per month for urban areas and 49 rupees ($6.33) per capita per month for rural areas between October 1973 and June 1974 using all-India urban and rural prices, respectively. The poverty ratio remained in the range of 45 percent to 50 percent and exceeded the 50 percent figure for some years.[28]

Political Mobilization and Democracy in India (London: Routledge, 2008), 78–89; Frankel, *India's Political Economy*, 388–490.

[27] Panagariya, *India: The Emerging Giant*, 59–71; Frankel, *India's Political Economy*, 434–90.

[28] Panagariya, *India: The Emerging Giant*, 133–6. The dollar figures reflect the rupee-dollar exchange rates in 1973. The conversion figures were obtained from http://fx.sauder.ubc.ca/etc/USDpages.pdf (accessed December 29, 2010).

Slow growth and unacceptable levels of absolute poverty coincided with a period when Prime Minister Gandhi's approach to politics can only be described as autocratic. The chapter on political mobilization describes how she undermined the democratic institutions within the Congress Party and the government of India (see Chapter 4). Efforts were made to initiate programs that would allow the central government to reach out to the poor directly, thereby circumventing state governments.[29] Political opposition in an increasingly mobilized society with few opportunities for employment, and in which institutional channels of interest articulation were constricted, generated social movements in states such as Bihar and Gujarat led by a charismatic socialist leader – Jayaprakash Narayan.[30]

Gradual Evolution of the Liberal Momentum: 1975–1990

In the mid-1970s, after years of sluggish economic growth accompanied by a poor record of human development, there was a gradual change in policy. Asian economies such as South Korea, Taiwan, and Singapore had demonstrated that private initiative and trade promotion could result in rapid economic growth and well-being. Most importantly, China's rise, powered by its export orientation since the late 1970s, was an even more convincing example of how integration with the

---

[29] Steven I. Wilkinson, "Explaining Changing Patterns of Party-Voter Linkages in India," in *Patrons, Clients, and Policies*, ed. Herbert Kitschelt and Steven I. Wilkinson (New York: Cambridge University Press, 2007), 113–18.

[30] Atul Kohli, *Democracy and Development in India* (New Delhi: Oxford University Press, 2009), 23–42; Hewitt, *Political Mobilization and Democracy in India*, 62–120. The student protests in Gujarat and Bihar during 1973 and 1974 and the strike of 1.7 million railway workers in 1974 posed serious threats to the government; see Frankel, *India's Political Economy 1947–2005*, 523–39.

world economy could benefit poor developing countries.[31] During this period, the government of India produced a number of important reports that were critical of its industrial regulations and suggested the urgent need to promote exports. These reports stressed the importance of industrial deregulation for enhancing the productivity and competitiveness of Indian industry.[32]

Industrialization

Indira Gandhi and later prime ministers – Rajiv Gandhi (October 1984–December 1989), Morarji Desai (March 1977–July 1979), Charan Singh (July 1979–January 1980), Vishwanath Pratap Singh (December 1989–November 1990), and Chandra Shekhar (November 1990–June 1991) – continued to gradually, and often stealthily, deregulate the

---

[31] Indira Gandhi, *Selected Speeches and Writings*, vol. 4 (New Delhi: Publications Division of the Ministry of Information and Broadcasting, November 1985), 236.

[32] For an overview of these reports, see P. N. Dhar, "The Indian Economy," in *The Indian Economy*, ed. Robert E. B. Lucas, and Gustave F. Papanek (New Delhi: Oxford University, 1988), 13–14. The important reports included P. C. Alexander (chair), *Report of the Committee on Import and Export Policies* (New Delhi: Ministry of Commerce, 1978); Vadilal Dagli, *Report of the Committee on Controls and Subsidies* (New Delhi: Ministry of Finance, 1978); Abid Hussain (chair), *Report of the Committee on Trade Policy* (New Delhi: Ministry of Commerce, 1984); M. Narasimham (chair), *Report on Industrial Licensing and Related MRTP Aspects* (New Delhi: Ministry of Finance, 1985). On the importance of the report by Lakshmi Kant Jha, *Report of the Commission on Economic and Administrative Reforms*, see Atul Kohli, "Politics of Economic Liberalization in India," *World Development* 17:3 (1989): 308. Scholars worried that India's manufacturing productivity needed to improve if India were to emulate the Asian success stories. For a review of these concerns in the academic literature apart from the government reports mentioned in the preceding text, see Mukherji, "The Political Economy of Reforms," 486–7; Isher J. Ahluwalia, *Productivity and Growth in Indian Manufacturing* (New Delhi: Oxford University Press, 1991); Marcel P. Timmer and Adam Szirmai, "Comparative Productivity Performance in Manufacturing in South and East Asia," *Oxford Development Studies* 27:1 (1999): 57–79.

economic activities of the private sector despite the persistence of socialist rhetoric. Rajiv Gandhi promoted the domestic private sector most actively.[33] Trade promotion was less successful than industrial deregulation during this period, and the ratio of India's trade to gross domestic product (GDP) stagnated between 1980 and 1990.[34] Various factions within the Congress Party vigorously contested the adoption of these policies. Additionally, powerful and entrenched interest groups such as industrialists, farmers, and bureaucrats had important stakes in maintaining a highly protected economy ridden with government controls.

The vast majority of Indian industrialists had become accustomed to exploiting the system of controls, in which licenses and approvals were required for production, imports and exports. Industrialists had become adept at the art of what Stanley Kochanek has aptly called "briefcase politics." Through their offices in Delhi, such industrialists maintained excellent relations with politicians and bureaucrats. A senior minister in Indira Gandhi's cabinet, Lalit Narayan Mishra, was notorious for receiving large sums of money in return for commercial privileges granted to industrialists.[35]

Not surprisingly, the pressure to promote industrial competitiveness rarely came from the business class. This class sought additional privileges to conduct business within the country but was unwilling to adjust to the risks of engaging

[33] On probusiness liberalization by stealth during this period, see Kohli, "The Politics of Economic Growth in India, 1980–2005: Part 1," 1251–9; and Panagariya, *India: The Emerging Giant*, 78–94. For a more general treatment of stealth and economic liberalization in India, see Rob Jenkins, *Democratic Politics and Economic Reform in India* (Cambridge: Cambridge University Press, 1999).

[34] The ratio of India's trade to GDP remained constant at 16% between 1980 and 1990. World Development Indicators, The World Bank, accessed through the National University of Singapore library Web site (accessed August 27, 2010).

[35] See Stanley Kochanek, "Liberalization and Business Lobbying in India," in *India's Economic Transition*, ed. Rahul Mukherji (New Delhi: Oxford University Press, 2007), 417–20.

with the global market. The Federation of Indian Chambers of Commerce and Industry (FICCI) was the most powerful industry organization in the early 1980s. It advised the government to reduce the import duty on intermediate goods and sought concessions for 100 percent export-oriented units. Yet it seemed unaware of India's export potential in the domains of information technology (IT) and pharmaceuticals. These industries, however, would soon emerge as the growth areas for the country's exports and the route to its integration with the global economy.[36]

The need for industrial reforms was understood by the technocracy and was promoted by the Prime Minister's Office (PMO).[37] The 1980 Industrial Policy Statement, under the premiership of Indira Gandhi, had charted a new direction. Schemes for expanding production capacity and initiating investment without government permission were more generous than the ones announced in 1975 and 1976.[38] Gandhi's most visible decision favoring a liberal policy outlook was to turn to the IMF for funds in the aftermath of the second oil shock of 1979. The government of India preempted the macroeconomic policy reforms that the IMF would have demanded and secured funds that were used largely to harness India's oil and natural gas reserves by developing the publicly

---

[36] FICCI, *Correspondence: 1981* (New Delhi: Federation House, 1981), 141–276. On business groups and other sources of political opposition to economic reforms during the 1980s, see Barnett R. Rubin, "Economic Liberalisation and the Indian State," *Third World Quarterly* 7:4 (1985): 742–57; Kohli, *Democracy and Development in India*, 186–225; James Manor, "Tried, and then Abandoned," *IDS Bulletin* 18:4 (1987): 39–44.

[37] For two excellent accounts of how the state promoted reforms in the 1980s, see Kohli, "Politics of Economic Liberalization in India," 305–28; E. Sridharan, "Economic Liberalization and India's Political Economy: Towards a Paradigm Synthesis," *Journal of Commonwealth and Comparative Politics* 31:3 (November 1993): 1–31.

[38] *Statement on Industrial Policy* (New Delhi: Department of Industrial Development – Ministry of Industry, July 1980); Panagariya, *India: The Emerging Giant*, 80–3.

owned Oil and Natural Gas Commission. Funds were finally
secured in 1981, despite severe criticism from the Reagan
administration and the Left parties in India. The IMF departed
from its orthodox approach of promoting privatization and
allowed a substantial proportion of the funds to be used to
strengthen the country's public-sector oil companies.[39] These
funds contributed to India's energy security, and consequently,
the country's ratio of oil imports to domestic production
declined from 60:40 to 30:70 within a period of five years.[40]

The gradual reduction of regulations for Indian industry
contributed to the acceleration in annual industrial growth,
from 4.5 percent during the period from 1961 to 1974 to
5.9 percent between 1975 and 1990.[41] The licensing process,
which involved obtaining government permission to enable
private companies to open industrial units in specified sectors, was being blatantly misused. Intellectual architects of
the licensing regime, such as the economist and technocrat
Indraprasad Gordhanbhai Patel, conceded in the mid-1980s
that policy makers had not expected that industrial licensing
would turn into a corruption racket.[42]

Factors such as a change in political leadership also
contributed to the process of economic reform. For example,
Rajiv Gandhi's premiership witnessed acceleration in the process of technological development and industrial deregulation

---

[39] John G. Ruggie, "Political Structure and Change in the International
Economic Order," in *Antinomies of Interdependence*, ed. John G. Ruggie
(New York: Columbia University Press, 1983), 458–9; Praveen
K. Chaudhry, Vijay L. Kelkar, and Vikash Yadav, "The Evolution
of 'Homegrown' Conditionality," *Journal of Development Studies*
40:6 (August 2004): 59–76; James Boughton, *Silent Revolution: The
International Monetary Fund 1979–89* (Washington, DC: International
Monetary Fund, 2001), 709–17.

[40] Catherine Gwin and Lawrence A. Veit, "The Indian Miracle," *Foreign
Policy* 58 (Spring 1985): 87.

[41] These figures are from the World Development Indicators, The World
Bank, accessed through the National University of Singapore library
Web site.

[42] I. G. Patel, "On Taking India into the Twenty-First Century," *Modern
Asian Studies* 21:2 (1987): 216–18.

in India. The prime minister was an airline pilot with a deep interest in electronics and radios.[43] First, under his watch, thirty industries and eighty-two pharmaceutical products were delicensed. Subsequently, under the premiership of Vishwanath Pratap Singh, investments up to 250 million rupees ($5.37 million) in developed regions and up to 750 million rupees ($16.12 million) in economically backward areas were delicensed.[44] Second, a policy of "broad banding" allowed firms to change the mix of products within an approved production capacity. For example, if a company had a license to produce fifty thousand high-powered motorcycles and sixty thousand fuel-efficient bikes, it had the leeway to adjust the production numbers between these two types of two-wheelers. Third, firms had earlier needed permission to produce more than the government-allocated production quota assigned to them, which was a disincentive for increasing production. The new policy allowed firms producing goods at the level of 80 percent plant efficiency to increase their production capacity to 133 percent. Finally, we have described how the MRTP had stringently controlled businesses with assets worth 200 million rupees or more ($4.3 million). Rajiv Gandhi's government raised that limit to 1 billion rupees ($21.5 million) and waived MRTP clearance for twenty-seven industries.[45]

In 1981, the government embarked upon a successful joint venture with the Suzuki Corporation of Japan, which gave birth to the Maruti car despite opposition from India's car manufacturers. This was followed by a new policy that allowed for automatic expansion of the production capacity in the automobile sector during 1985. The successful production and marketing of the Maruti Suzuki car was a landmark achievement in improving the efficiency and reliability of Indian cars.

---

[43] Dinesh C. Sharma, *The Long Revolution* (New Delhi: HarperCollins, 2009), 124–73.
[44] Panagariya, *India: The Emerging Giant*, 99–100.
[45] Ibid., 83–5, 98–109. See also Kohli, *Democracy and Development in India*, 147–63; Nayar, "When Did the Hindu Rate of Growth End?" 1887–90.

Two automobiles had dominated the Indian market until the mid-1980s: the Fiat under the brand name Premier Padmini, which was a version of the Fiat 1100 and was very popular in India from the 1950s onward, and the Hindustan Ambassador, which was a version of the Morris Oxford III model produced by the Morris Motor Company in 1956. Suzuki's technology and reliability challenged these two existing brands, which had so long monopolized Indian roads. Deregulation in the automobile sector during the 1980s also became the basis for the realization of comparative advantage in the automobile components sector in the years ahead.[46]

Furthermore, problems relating to the provision of physical infrastructure were also addressed. Throughout the 1980s, telecommunications services and the manufacture of telephone switches were deregulated. A Department of Telecommunications (DOT) was created in 1985 within the Ministry of Communications in order to focus on enhancing the quality of telecommunications services. A government-owned corporate entity, Mahanagar Telecom Nigam Limited (MTNL), was created to serve the metropolises of Delhi and Mumbai in 1986. However, political opposition from the DOT ensured that MTNL was not allowed to operate in any other Indian city.[47]

Other institutional innovations followed. For example, the Centre for the Development of Telematics was created as an autonomous agency within the government in 1984. It successfully produced the switch technology for telephone exchanges in rural areas after competing with multinationals such as Alcatel. Innovation within a government department was licensed for the first time to private manufacturers, who were given licenses to produce telephone switches.[48]

[46] Subir Gokarn, Anindya Sen, and Rajendra R. Vaidya, *The Structure of Indian Industry* (New Delhi: Oxford University Press, 2004), 281–96.

[47] Rahul Mukherji, "Managing Competition," in Mukherji, *India's Economic Transition*, 301–4.

[48] Ibid. See J. P. Singh, *Leapfrogging Development* (Albany: State University of New York Press, 1999), 141–63; M. B. Athreya, "India's Telecommunications Policy," *Telecommunications Policy* 20:1 (January

The 1980s also witnessed the birth of comparative advantage in India's IT sector. This was the first commercial activity that earned the country's service trade a good reputation. First, English education, good engineering colleges, and institutions of higher learning in the sciences, coupled with low wages, produced a natural comparative advantage in IT services. Second, the FERA described earlier in this chapter had restricted foreign equity in Indian companies to 40 percent, whereas a 51 percent equity share was required for substantial powers over a company's decision making. This led to the exit of companies such as IBM, which freed substantial talent for India's first generation of middle-class entrepreneurs and managers.[49] Third, scientists and technocrats rather than career civil servants increasingly came to dominate the Department of Electronics under the aegis of the PMO. These technocrats supported the qualified engineer entrepreneurs in the IT sector and pursued a policy of gradual deregulation. Easier imports of computers and software to facilitate exports became possible because of the support of these technocrats. However, the Ministry of Finance, which was concerned about revenue losses due to lowered customs duties, opposed the efforts of the Department of Electronics.[50]

Agriculture

Other parts of the Indian economy also showed signs of improvement during the 1990s. For example, the agricultural

1996): 11–17; on the success of the Centre for Development of Telematics, see Evans, *Embedded Autonomy*, 134–5.

[49] Joseph M. Grieco, *Between Dependency and Autonomy: India's Experience with the International Computer Industry* (Berkeley: University of California Press, 1984), 16–52.

[50] On how the 1980s prepared the IT sector for a boom in the 1990s, see Vibha Pingle, *Rethinking the Developmental State* (New Delhi: Oxford University Press, 1999), 126–41; AnnaLee Saxenian, "Bangalore," in Mukherji, *India's Economic Transition*, 361–9; Evans, *Embedded Autonomy*, 113–16, 168–73. On why the electronics industry did not take a similar route, see E. Sridharan, *The Political Economy of Industrial Promotion* (Westport, CT: Praeger, 1996), 113–56.

sector registered an annual growth rate of 3.4 percent in the 1980s, which was higher than that witnessed in any other decade after the country's independence.[51] After the Janata government came to power in 1977 (1977–9), farmers successfully pressured the Ministry of Agriculture to take a generous view of agricultural pricing. Charan Singh, who was a senior minister within the Janata Party, went on to become the prime minister during a brief period between July 1979 and January 1980. He had fought for the interests of farmers since the 1950s. Although the Janata government was short-lived, profarmer procurement prices and subsidies initiated during this period held sway for the entire decade.[52]

Leaders of powerful farming lobbies such as Mahendra Singh Tikait, Sharad Joshi, and M. D. Nanjundaswamy kept up the pressure on the government. They convincingly argued that urban India had neglected rural areas for too long. Tikait and the Indian Farmer's Union were powerful in the populous state of Uttar Pradesh and enjoyed considerable influence in the western states of Punjab and Haryana. It fought against the excesses of moneylenders and middlemen who reduced the profit margins of farmers. Joshi, who was from the western and industrialized state of Maharashtra, argued for an end to the policy bias against agriculture and for strengthening rural markets. Nanjundaswamy worked with farmers in the southern state of Karnataka (Karnataka Rajya Rayatu Sangha), and he was ideologically opposed to the market. These farmers' movements successfully and continually put pressure on the government to offer generous procurement prices for food grains such as wheat and rice and to subsidize agricultural inputs.[53]

[51] S. Mahendra Dev, *Inclusive Growth in India* (New York: Oxford University Press, 2008), 28.

[52] On the difference made by the growing power of the farmer's lobby to agricultural policy see Varshney, *Democracy, Development and the Countryside*, 81–145.

[53] On farmer's movements in India, see Gail Omvedt, "Farmer's Movements," in *Social Movements in India*, ed. Raka Ray and Mary

Human Development

Industrial and agricultural development during the 1980s made some impact on economic well-being. However, these efforts were rather dismal in the face of the high levels of economic deprivation that were prevalent in India. First, India's success in the area of higher education has been accompanied with unacceptable levels of illiteracy and poverty. The government paid little heed to these shortcomings and even argued in favor of child labor, arguing that it might be necessary for the survival of poverty-stricken families.[54]

A few notable policies were initiated after 1975 that would work to reverse this trend. Realizing that education had suffered partly because it was governed exclusively by the states within the Indian Union, Indira Gandhi chose to amend the Indian constitution in 1976. Subsequently, education was moved from the list of subjects governed by Indian states to one that would be governed concurrently by the central government and the states. The National Policy on Education (1986) and the National Literacy Mission (1988) initiated by Rajiv Gandhi were significant attempts to make an impact on the eradication of illiteracy.[55] India's literacy rate rose from 43.5 percent in 1981 to 52.2 percent in 1991.[56]

Second, the promotion of public health attracted less policy attention and resources compared with literacy programs in India. Although the country spent 2.96 percent of its GDP on education, the same figure for health was 0.72 percent in

F. Katzenstein (New Delhi: Oxford University Press, 2005), 185–90; Akhil Gupta, *Postcolonial Developments* (Durham, NC: Duke University Press, 1998), 62–101.

[54] Myron Weiner, *The Child and the State in India* (New Delhi: Oxford University Press, 1991).

[55] Nilekani, *Imagining India: Ideas for the New Century* (New Delhi: Penguin Allen Lane, 2008), 196–9; Jandhyala B. G. Tilak, "Universalizing Elementary Education," in *Universalizing Elementary Education in India* (New Delhi: Oxford University Press, 2009), 41–50.

[56] Government of India, *Economic Survey 2008/09* (New Delhi: Oxford University Press, 2009), A122.

1980 and 1981.[57] India has suffered from high levels of health-worker absenteeism because of a system of incentives that provided for a regular fixed salary that was unrelated to the number of patients treated by a doctor.[58] Compulsory service for doctors in rural areas could not be implemented. Most doctors opted for specialized training rather than preventive and social medicine.[59]

Third, there was no significant decline in the proportion of Indians living below the poverty line until 1973. The number of people below the official poverty line, which was 45.31 percent in the fiscal year 1950–1, rose to 46.54 percent in 1961–2, and increased to 53.37 percent in 1972–3. But this figure kept steadily declining to 43 percent in 1983–4 and to 35.49 percent in 1990–1.[60] The gradual deregulation of the economy probably accounts for this reduction in overall poverty rates.

The Roots of a Financial Crisis

The previous section describes the rising investments and initiatives in industrial, infrastructural, agricultural, and human development in India during the 1980s. Yet, unlike in many Asian economies, trade and foreign direct investment were not used as a way of generating resources for development. India's trade as a percentage of its GDP, which was 16 percent in 1980, remained at the same level in 1990. The comparable figures for China were 22 percent and 35 percent, respectively.[61] The import of the success of Asian economies

---

[57] Nayar, *The Myth of the Shrinking State*, 86–92.

[58] Jeffrey Hammer, Yamini Aiyar, and Salimah Samji, "Understanding Government Failure in Public Health Services," *Economic and Political Weekly* 42:40 (October 6, 2007): 4049–57.

[59] Roger Jeffrey, *The Politics of Health in India* (Berkeley: University of California Press, 1988), 129, 143–88.

[60] Panagariya, *India: The Emerging Giant*, 131–6.

[61] These figures are from the World Development Indicators, The World Bank, accessed through the National University of Singapore library Web site (accessed September 29, 2009).

such as Japan, South Korea, Taiwan, and Singapore and, most recently, rapid economic growth in China was not lost on Indian policy makers. The country had failed to discipline capital and change the orientation of its economy away from import substitution toward export-led growth.[62] It was the mismatch between resource mobilization and the government's expenditures in the context of a closed economy that produced the 1991 balance-of-payments crisis.

Industrialists, farmers, and the urban middle classes were making demands on the state's exchequer during the 1980s. Rising demands from an increasingly mobilized society, described in Chapter 4, had led to a growing deficit between government expenditure and revenue.[63] The government became increasingly dependent on commercial sources of borrowing in order to fund this deficit.

By 1990, a financial crisis was looming large over India. Given the growth of spending by the government, the fiscal deficit increased as a proportion of its GDP from 8.1 percent between the fiscal years 1980–1 and 1984–5 to 10.1 percent between the fiscal years 1985–6 and 1989–90. The growth areas of government expenditure included interest payments on commercial borrowings, subsidies for targeted beneficiaries in agriculture and industry, and defense expenditure.[64] This pattern of spending reflected a political economy in which the farmer, industrialist, and urban middle class exerted pressure for concessions. The government was forced to acquiesce to these pressures. Moreover, the social mobilization of erstwhile backward and untouchable classes meant that state

---

[62] On the impact of China, see Jalal Alamgir, *India's Open Economy Policy* (New York: Routledge, 2009), 89–120. Montek S. Ahluwalia, the Deputy Chairman of India's Planning Commission since 2004, confirmed this view (author interview, New Delhi, January 5, 2005).

[63] On the relationship between increasing level of political and social mobilization and the fiscal deficit, see Rahul Mukherji, "Economic Transition in a Plural Polity: India," in Mukherji, *India's Economic Transition*, 119–26.

[64] Ibid., 126–8; Joshi and Little, *India: Macroeconomics and Political Economy*, 225–35.

and central governments had to pay greater heed to a larger number of interest groups than in the past.[65]

Government expenditures had increased substantially at a time when India had become excessively dependent on commercial borrowings. Commercial banks did not view the ever-rising fiscal deficit in a positive light and became more concerned about political uncertainty when Rajiv Gandhi was succeeded first by Vishwanath Pratap Singh in December 1989 and, soon thereafter, by Chandra Shekhar in November 1990. Furthermore, the issue of implementing populist measures such as the recommendations of the Mandal Commission (1980), which prescribed the reservation of 27 percent of the seats in institutions of higher learning and in government jobs for other backward classes,[66] in addition to the 22 percent reserved for scheduled castes and tribes, was raised for the first time during the premiership of Vishwanath Pratap Singh.[67] Foreign commercial banks worried that these populist policies would have an adverse impact on India's finances and its creditworthiness.

The Gulf War occurred at a time when populist politics and policies had generated an expanding fiscal deficit. The crisis arising from Iraq's invasion of Kuwait in August 1990 and the consequent rapid rise in the price of oil between August and October hurt the Indian exchequer to the tune of 1 percent of India's GDP. A substantial downgrade in Moody's credit rating from A2 (good ability to pay) to Ba2

---

[65] On social and political mobilizations in the 1980s, see Francine Frankel, "Decline of a Social Order," in *Politics in India*, ed. Sudipta Kaviraj (New Delhi: Oxford University Press, 1997), 370–82; Lloyd I. Rudolph and Susanne H. Rudolph, *In Pursuit of Lakshmi* (Chicago: University of Chicago Press, 1987), 228–44, Kohli, *Democracy and Development in India*, 23–42; Ashutosh Varshney, "Is India Becoming More Democratic?" *Journal of Asian Studies* 59:1 (February 2000): 3–25; Christophe Jaffrelot, "The Rise of the Other Backward Classes in the Hindi Belt," *Journal of Asian Studies* 59:1 (February 2000): 86–108; Sumit Ganguly, *The Crisis in Kashmir* (Cambridge: Cambridge University Press, 1997), 14–42.

[66] A good description of the other backward classes is in Chapter 4.

[67] Frankel, *India's Political Economy*, 688–89.

(speculative) between June 1990 and March 1991 led to the shutting down of all credit windows.[68] Moody's highlighted India's high debt-to-service payment ratio, high dependence on commercial borrowing, and high debt-to-export ratio as reasons for downgrading its sovereign rating.[69]

The autarkic orientation of the private sector and the demand for higher subsidies by all groups became unsustainable in the context of a rather closed economy with substantial industrial controls. A fiscal crisis that was turning into a serious balance-of-payments crisis for the first time after 1966 helped constituencies within the government that wished for India to promote competitiveness more vigorously and engage with the global economy.

A leaked confidential paper circulated within the PMO and authored by Montek Singh Ahluwalia in June 1990 was the most visible sign of desperation among the proliberalizing technocrats.Vishwanath Pratap Singh had visited Malaysia with Ahluwalia in 1990 and was surprised to find that the country had developed far more rapidly than India within a short period of time.[70] He urged Ahluwalia to draft an agenda for economic reforms at a time when the balance-of-payments crisis was around the corner. In the paper, "Towards Restructuring Industrial, Trade and Fiscal Policies," Ahluwalia drew the blueprint for radical economic reform in India. The paper recommended tariff reduction, greater freedom for foreign capital, a 20 percent devaluation of the rupee, the closure of unviable public-sector units, and raising the MRTP

---

[68] Ephraim Clark and Geeta Lakshmi, "Controlling the Risk: A Case Study of the Indian Liquidity Crisis 1990–92," *Journal of International Development* 15:3 (March 2003): 285–98; Joshi and Little, *India: Macroeconomics and Political Economy*, 65–7.

[69] Joshi and Little, *India: Macroeconomics and Political Economy*, 180–9; Amit Bhaduri and Deepak Nayyar, *An Intelligent Person's Guide to Liberalization* (New Delhi: Penguin Books, 1996), 24–30.

[70] Ahluwalia was a secretary in the PMO at this time. He is one of the architects of India's economic reforms and has served as the deputy chairman of the Planning Commission since 2004 and holds the rank of a cabinet minister in India.

asset limit substantially.[71] The agenda for economic reform had arrived in the 1980s, although the political conditions necessary for change would not be available until the 1991 balance-of-payments crisis.

The Consolidation and Sustenance of the Liberal Economy: The Indian Economy after 1991

We have described how Indian technocrats and statesmen had attempted to improve conditions for private business in India during the 1980s. They made limited progress in improving the conditions for entrepreneurship and had achieved considerably less in the area of trade promotion. The political economy of growth and development after 1975 had produced a grave fiscal situation, and the consequent dependence on foreign commercial banks was financially unsustainable after May 1991. It was this economic crisis that empowered liberal statesmen and technocrats to move the Indian economy substantially in the direction of private entrepreneurship and economic globalization after 1991. The 1980s had prepared the ground for this ideational shift. It is in this sense that 1991 marks a watershed in India's economic history.

This section will first describe why significant economic reforms occurred after 1991. Second, what were the significant changes in trade and industrial policies, and what was their impact on domestic and foreign firms? Third, why did the infrastructure in telecommunications, stock markets, and airlines become efficient? Fourth, what are the major challenges to development that still need to be addressed?

Why Did Substantial Reforms Occur after 1991?

The foreign-exchange crisis forced India to approach the IMF for conditional lending in June 1991. The government

---

[71] See Vanita Shastri, "The Politics of Economic Liberalization in India," *Contemporary South Asia* 6:1 (1997): 43–4.

had explored other sources of funding to meet its import obligations. It had even shipped gold to the Union Bank of Switzerland and the Bank of England in order to obtain foreign exchange. Commercial banks decided to stop lending to India; nonresident Indians, whose deposits in India could have been used to meet the country's foreign-exchange obligations, began withdrawing their savings. The option for India was either to default on its import payments or seek conditional resources from the IMF. A default would have affected its substantial imports of oil and intermediate goods, and it would have been exceedingly difficult to manage the economy without essential imports.[72]

This dire crisis prompted a firm resolve within the technocracy to promote India's competitiveness and its private sector. Greater support for economic deregulation and trade promotion among economists and technocrats existed in 1991 than was the case in 1966. The crisis also helped the reformer technocrats to deal with the opponents of reforms. Rajiv Gandhi's assassination in May 1991 increased the resolve of the Congress Party, which came to power in June that year, to leverage the crisis and fulfill the late prime minister's vision.

P.V. Narasimha Rao, who became prime minister in 1991, understood that he was confronted with a unique situation in India's economic history. The Cold War had ended at a time when India was facing a financial crisis. Its dependence on the Soviet Union for markets and imports needed to be restructured. This was also an opportunity for India to chart a new course of economic engagement with Asia, the United States, and parts of the Western world, which had benefited from global economic interdependence during the Cold War.[73] Rao invited a technocrat, Dr. Manmohan Singh, to serve as finance minister. Singh had appreciated the importance of

---

[72] On the severity of the crisis, see Bhaduri and Nayyar, *The Intelligent Person's Guide to Liberalization*, 22–30.

[73] I am grateful to the late Prime Minister Rao for these insights (author interview, New Delhi, February 2001).

global economic interdependence when he was writing his doctoral dissertation at Oxford during the early 1960s. His thesis had suggested that India needed to promote its exports at a time when import substitution rather than export promotion was the dominant policy paradigm.[74] Technocrats, who favored greater private-sector and trade orientation and had gained enormous policy experience in the 1980s, including Montek Singh Ahluwalia, C. Rangarajan, Rakesh Mohan, and Raja Chelliah,[75] enjoyed the support of the prime minister. They made a virtue of the crisis to guide the economy toward greater reliance on markets and trade.

The more professionally inclined parts of Indian industry aided the process of economic reform. Rajiv Gandhi had worked closely with the Association of Indian Engineering Industry (AIEI) to increase its profile in relation to the preeminent Indian industry association, the FICCI. He had favored the AIEI over the FICCI and convinced the AIEI leadership to change its name to the Confederation of Indian Industry (CII). The CII's Secretary General Tarun Das worked with the segments of Indian industry that were more favorably

[74] See Manmohan Singh, *India's Export Trends* (Oxford: Clarendon Press, 1964). Amartya Sen has argued that this was quite an exceptional argument at that time; see Amartya Sen, "Theory and Practice of Development," in *India's Economic Reforms and Development*, ed. Isher J. Ahluwalia and I. M. D. Little (New Delhi: Oxford University Press, 1998), 73–84.

[75] Ahluwalia was commerce secretary during 1990 and 1991 and secretary in the Ministry of Finance from 1991–8; Rangarajan was a member of the Planning Commission in 1991 and served as governor of the Reserve Bank from 1991–7; Mohan served as an adviser in the Ministry of Finance from 1991–7; and Chelliah chaired the Tax Reforms Committee from 1991–3 and served as fiscal adviser in the Ministry of Finance from 1993–5. These reformers had served the government with distinction during the 1980s. E.g., Montek Ahluwalia had served the Ministry of Finance (1979–85), had served the PMO (1985–90), and was secretary in the Department of Commerce (1990–1) at the time of the balance-of-payments crisis. For details about Ahluwalia's career see the Planning Commission Web site, http://planningcommission.nic.in/aboutus/history/msapro.htm (accessed December 22, 2010).

inclined toward reforms after 1991. Moreover, Indian industrialists, the majority of whom favored the protected Indian market, needed resources to finance imports. The only option available in the short run was to acquiesce to reforms that the IMF and the technocracy had imposed upon them.[76]

The IMF was fairly respectful of the views of the Indian technocrats whose ideas had evolved significantly during the 1980s. The IMF thereby allowed the technocracy to deviate from orthodox programs to a greater extent than it usually allowed when imposing stabilization programs on a country. Labor laws were not restructured, and India was allowed to run fiscal deficits in excess of what the IMF thought was optimal beyond the first year of the program.[77]

Economic Reforms and Industrialization in India

The results of the reform program were noteworthy. Substantial tariff liberalization, especially in intermediate goods,

[76] On the evolution of the relationship between AIEI, CII, and the government of India, see Kochanek, "Liberalization and Business Lobbying in India," 424–7; Jorgen D. Pederson, "Explaining Economic Liberalization in India," *World Development* 28:2 (2000): 268–71; Aseema Sinha, "Understanding the Rise and Transformation of Business Collective Action in India," *Business and Politics* 7:2 (2005): 1–27; Sharmila Kantha and Shubhajyoti Roy, *Building India with Partnership: The Story of CII* (New Delhi: Penguin Books, 2006), 139–87. I am grateful to Chief Mentor Tarun Das at CII for valuable insights and for introducing me to the people who steer the organization (author interview, New Delhi, June 3, 2009). For business opposition to the 1991 reforms, see Alamgir, *India's Open Economy Policy*, 31–3. I am indebted to D. H. Pai Panandiker, secretary general of the FICCI during 1991, for his views on the matter (author interview, New Delhi, June 2, 2009).

[77] I am indebted to discussions with Jagdish Bhagwati, university professor at Columbia University, a person outside the government who played an important role during the crisis episode (author interview, New York City, November 14, 1997); Montek S. Ahluwalia (author interview, New Delhi, January 5, 2005); Vijay L. Kelkar (author interview, Mumbai, January 3, 2005); and Rakesh Mohan (author interview, Mumbai, January 3, 2005). Ahluwalia, Kelkar, and Mohan had been influential technocrats involved with the reform process.

was accompanied with the significant devaluation of the Indian rupee. Tariff liberalization reduced the cost of inputs and pressured Indian industry to become more competitive. The devaluation of the rupee increased the cost of imports and reduced the price of Indian exports.[78] The net effective protection enjoyed by domestic industry was thus reduced to a much-lesser extent than what the magnitude of tariff reduction would suggest. Indian products immediately became more competitive due to the currency devaluation. This was a major boon for export-oriented sectors like IT. India's merchandise exports doubled once between 1991 and 1999, and again between 2002 and 2003 and between 2005 and 2006. Its IT and service exports doubled between 2004 and 2005 and between 2005 and 2006.[79]

FERA, which had restricted foreign equity to a maximum limit of 40 percent, was replaced with a regime that allowed 51 percent foreign equity in most sectors of the economy. India consequently attracted much-greater foreign investment than in the past. It received $24 billion worth of investment through the foreign direct-investment route between 1992 and 2002 − an improvement on the past, but a figure that China could surpass in a single year. However, Indian companies still remained largely averse to foreign investment.[80]

Some exceptions existed, though. First, the IT sector, which is highly competitive, accepted the presence of foreign capital. Second, smaller companies that needed foreign capital, technology, and managerial expertise in order to compete with larger entities welcomed foreign capital as joint-venture partners. They have successfully opposed the aversion of larger Indian

---

[78] On trade reforms see Suresh D. Tendulkar and T. A. Bhavani, *Understanding Reforms: Post-1991 India* (New Delhi: Oxford University Press, 2007), 116–25.

[79] Panagariya, *India: The Emerging Giant*, 262. For an account of the political economy of India's trade policy, see Vinod K. Aggarwal and Rahul Mukherji, "India's Shifting Trade Policy," in *Asia's New Institutional Architecture*, ed. Vinod K. Aggarwal and Min Gyo Koo (Heidelberg, Germany: Springer-Verlag, 2008), 215–58.

[80] Tendulkar and Bhavani, *Understanding Reforms: Post-1991 India*, 106–16.

industrialists toward foreign investors. For example, an increase in the foreign-equity limit in Indian telecommunications was welcomed by Bharati Enterprises, whose telecommunications company, Airtel, has benefited enormously from its partnerships with Singtel, Warburg Pincus, and other foreign companies. It has emerged as India's largest telecommunications company. This is in contrast to its cash-rich competitors, including Tata Telecom and Reliance Infocomm, who have been opposed to the entry of foreign capital into India's telecommunications sector.[81] The result is that India has attracted more than $20 billion a year in foreign investment since 2006.[82]

The availability of abundant entrepreneurial resources aided the process of promoting India's competitiveness in many areas after 1991. The country's largest private firm, the Tata Group, valued at $63 billion in 2008, has transformed itself into a multinational company. Its global sales for the year ending March 2008 represented 61 percent of its total sales, and 30 percent of the group's 350,000 employees reside outside India. Ratan Tata, the head of the Tata Group, transformed the Tata companies in two significant ways after 1991. First, he decided to enhance the productivity of the Tata companies. For example, Tata Steel successfully negotiated a voluntary retirement scheme for thirty thousand workers and invested $2.5 billion in capital upgrading in order to propel the company from a "top fifty" corporation to a "top five" steel company in the world. Second, it pursued an aggressive strategy of globalization. Its purchase of the Anglo-Dutch company Corus Steel for $12.1 billion in 2007 was one of the largest deals in the history of the steel industry. Tata Steel's strategy was to link low-cost production in India with Corus's

---

[81] Rahul Mukherji, "The Politics of Telecommunications Regulation: State-Industry Alliance Favoring Foreign Investment in India," *Journal of Development Studies* 44:10 (November 2008): 1405–23.

[82] This figure is from the World Development Indicators, The World Bank, accessed through the National University of Singapore library Web site (accessed August 3, 2010).

high-quality products. Other major Tata Group buys that are
designed to aid its foray into the international market include
the purchase of Tetley, the second-largest selling tea brand in
2000, and automobile brands such as Jaguar and Land Rover in
2008. Globalization requires significant innovation. Not only
has Tata Motors produced a successful Indian car (Indica), it
has also introduced a new concept in the automobile industry
through its Nano, which is the world's cheapest car (priced
at $2,500). The Nano has catapulted the Tata Group to the
sixth position among the world's most innovative companies
according to *Business Week* – behind Apple, Google, Toyota,
General Electric, and Microsoft, and ahead of Sony, Nokia,
IBM, and BMW.[83]

Another example of a successful global player in the area of
manufacturing is Bharat Forge. It produces machine components used by the world's top auto makers, and is the second-
largest forging company in the world, behind ThyssenKrupp
of Germany and ahead of Sumitomo Metal of Japan. By
the late 1980s, the company had emerged as a leader within
India under the regime of industrial controls. Chairman
and Managing Director Baba Kalyani turned a company
that depended on low-skilled manpower using rudimentary
mechanization to one that used skilled professionals and state-
of-the-art technology. The company has made significant foreign acquisitions that have helped it to access technology and
penetrate markets. Its manufacturing locations include three
in India, three in Germany, two in China, and one each in
North America, Sweden, and Scotland as of 2008.[84]

At another level, middle-class Indian entrepreneurs such as
Narayan Murthy and Nandan Nilekani of Infosys took advantage of deregulation and India's emerging natural comparative
advantage in the software and services sector during the 1980s.
Infosys, which had been founded on a $250 initial investment

[83] Nirmalya Kumar, *India's Global Powerhouses* (Boston: Harvard Business
Press, 2009), 157–76.
[84] Ibid., 83–94.

by a group of talented engineers in 1981, had transformed into a \$4 billion company by 2008. Its comparative advantage was based on its low-cost and skilled English-speaking engineers, who had been trained in India's engineering colleges. Infosys was an early global player, but struggled with software export in the late 1980s. Its sales were less than half a million dollars in 1989, and one of the founders left the company at that time.

The devaluation of the rupee and substantial reduction in import controls after 1991 enabled companies like Infosys to become global brands. Infosys followed the strategy of adopting sound corporate governance by submitting itself to the standards set by the NASDAQ,[85] as well as by accepting the United States' Generally Accepted Accounting Principles. Excellent corporate governance and commitment to its clients won the company a good brand name. The talent of its entrepreneurs lay in locating the bulk of the company's work in India at a low cost and in moving the bare minimum of client servicing to foreign destinations. The Infosys Centre in Mysore (southern India) is one of the largest software-oriented human-resource development facilities in the world and is capable of training fourteen thousand people every quarter. In 2007, the company accepted a mere 3 percent of the candidates from a pool of 1.3 million applicants.[86]

Promoting Provision of Efficient Infrastructure

This section describes the manner in which structural reform that promoted efficiency in various key infrastructure sectors

[85] NASDAQ originally stood for National Association of Securities Dealers Automated Quotations Systems, but the exchange's official stance is that the acronym is obsolete. It is the largest electronic screen–based equity securities trading market in the United States and the fourth largest by market capitalization in the world.

[86] Kumar, *India's Global Powerhouses*, 64–82; Tarun Khanna, *Billions of Entrepreneurs* (Boston: Harvard Business School Press, 2007), 122–6. See also http://www.indianexpress.com/news/sonia-inaugurates-infosys-gecii-in-mysore/517341/ (accessed August 3, 2010).

was consolidated in India. India's stock markets, telecommunications sector, and private airlines have changed beyond recognition in the postreform period. In most cases, the requisite political will to promote efficiency at the time of a looming financial crisis helped discipline these sectors and made them more productive.

First, India's stock-market reforms have been significant. These markets have attracted foreign and Indian savings that were critical for the growth of the country's corporate sector. India received $24 billion each from foreign direct and portfolio investment between 1992 and 2002.[87] Indian stock markets also began to attract the savings of Indian nationals living abroad because they offered the promise of higher returns. A financial crisis was necessary but not sufficient to engender reforms in the governance of India's stock markets. The old regime had resisted computerization and electronic trading and had continued with an opaque system of the settlement of transactions that favored the established brokers of the Bombay Stock Exchange (BSE). In the late 1980s, brokers had successfully resisted the reforms attempted by the president of the BSE, Mahendra Kampani. The Ministry of Finance had hoped that the BSE would reform itself in the aftermath of the 1991 balance-of-payments crisis. When reforms were not forthcoming, it decided to set up the National Stock Exchange (NSE) in 1993. The Ministry of Finance possesses substantial powers to set up a new stock market. Moreover, brokers were cash rich but did not have electoral clout. These strategic advantages aided the ministry to challenge the BSE by setting up the NSE.[88] The NSE had become the largest stock exchange in India by 1995 and in turn spurred reforms in the BSE. All the country's stock exchanges were subsequently computerized by 1999.

[87] Tendulkar and Bhavani, *Understanding Reforms: Post-1991 India*, 111–12.

[88] John Echeverri-Gent, "Politics of Market Micro-Structure: Towards a New Political Economy of India's Equity Market Reform," in Mukherji, *India's Economic Transition*, 331–50.

Reforms in trading norms, however, had to wait until 2003. The power of the old brokers was so strong that it was only after a major stock-market scam in 2001 that trading rules were made transparent owing to pressure from the Ministry of Finance.

Second, the success of India's stock market was surpassed by the boom in Indian telecommunications. This sector has recorded a growth rate that has outstripped that of other countries. Telephone connections in India zoomed from approximately 23 million in 1999 to about 672 million in 2010. Of the 672 million telephone lines installed in 2010, 617.5 million were mobile phones. The private sector served approximately 85 percent of India's telecommunications market in 2010. Although the disparity between rural and urban mobile connections is substantial, mobile phones are also serving the rural areas.[89] Connectivity is as much a boon for the rich as it is for the poor. Construction workers, farmers, vegetable sellers, and cab drivers have benefited from the telecommunication revolution as much as the high-technology and knowledge-intensive service industries. Developments in cellular technology, which was less capital-intensive and relatively free from regulatory bottlenecks, boosted the growth of this industry.

Reforms during the 1990s promoted private-sector participation in the Indian telecommunications industry. In the 1990s, the DOT resisted private-sector participation in two ways. First, it allowed private participation only in areas that it thought did not have significant business potential. Exclusive private-sector participation was allowed in mobile telephony based on this assumption. Second, bidding procedures and taxation rendered the business environment adverse for private players. However, private-sector participation was promoted by the PMO, often with the support of the Ministry

---

[89] These figures for June 30, 2010 were obtained from the Web site of the Telecom Regulatory Authority of India. See http://www.trai.gov.in/WriteReadData/trai/upload/PressReleases/746/PressRelease23july.pdf (accessed December 29, 2010).

of Finance. It was these institutions that aided the process of consolidation of the Telecom Regulatory Authority of India and the Telecom Dispute Settlement Appellate Tribunal. The two bodies were designed to create a level playing field for public- and private-sector telephone operators.

Prime Minister Atal Bihari Vajpayee (1998–2004) was able to nudge the system toward independent regulation at the time of the investment crises in 1997 and 2000. The DOT, as the regulator and service provider, had devised rules that were hurting the private sector financially. A serious crisis relating to investment for private telecommunications companies existed in 1999 after the government-owned company Mahanagar Telephone Nigam Limited was allowed license fee–free entry into the cellular business in 1998. Government-owned financial organizations that had given loans to the private sector also suffered losses in the process. The initiatives of Prime Minister Vajpayee at this time enabled regulatory institutions to become more independent in settling disputes between private companies and government-owned telecommunications providers. As mentioned earlier, privately owned Airtel is India's largest service provider; government-owned companies such as MTNL and BSNL have become efficient in response to competition and serve large parts of the rural market.[90]

Third, private airlines were permitted to operate in India after 1994. The 1994 Air Corporations Act was a significant departure from an earlier act governing civil aviation since 1953, which had nationalized civil aviation. During the post-liberalization era, airlines such as Jet, Kingfisher, Air Deccan,

---

[90] On India's telecommunications transformation, see Ashok V. Desai, *India's Telecommunications Industry* (New Delhi: Sage Publications, 2006); Rahul Mukherji, "Interests, Wireless Technology and Institutional Change: From Government Monopoly to Regulated Competition in Indian Telecommunications," *The Journal of Asian Studies* 68:2 (May 2009): 491–517. BSNL stands for Bharat Sanchar Nigam Limited, which is the government-owned telecom service provider serving all of India except Delhi and Mumbai.

Indigo, and Spice Jet serve a variety of customers, both high-end and low-end, on domestic and international routes. Air traffic has surged from approximately thirteen million in 2000 to thirty-seven million passengers in 2008. However, the airlines sector still lacks an independent regulator.[91] Although competition has resulted in a significant reduction in fares, the government-owned carrier Air India continues to record substantial losses. An independent regulator that can subject Air India to the pressures of competition has become imperative for realizing the competitive potential of this sector.[92]

Developmental Challenges

The successful industrial, trade, and infrastructure reforms described in the preceding text have not had the desired impact on substantial parts of the Indian economy. Electricity generation, which is critical for industry, agricultural growth, and the general well-being of citizens, is a matter of serious policy concern. Although there has been some success in the area of literacy and poverty alleviation, India still lags behind in these areas. The country's record in the area of nutrition is cause for even greater concern. The disparity in economic growth and development among Indian states grew exponentially after 1991, and the poorest parts of the country, with low levels of human development, are also the regions where the majority of Indians reside.

The failure of India's power sector to provide services efficiently stands in sharp contrast to the success of the country's telecommunications sector. The electricity boards run by the state governments are losing money. The net subsidy burden increased from 221.2 billion rupees ($4.75 billion) in 2005 and 2006 to 327.2 billion rupees ($7.03 billion) in 2008 and

---

[91] Panagariya, *India: The Emerging Giant*, 397–401.
[92] Rahul Mukherji and Gaurav Kankanhalli, "Civil Aviation in India," Working Paper 97 (Singapore: Institute of South Asian Studies, November 18, 2009): 1–18.

2009.[93] Two kinds of problems affect efficient service delivery in this sector. First, politically powerful farmers are unwilling to pay for electricity. Chief ministers of states such as Andhra Pradesh and Tamil Nadu, which lack abundant groundwater resources, routinely acquiesce to these demands. Second, there is rampant theft of electricity. States such as Andhra Pradesh have shown some progress in reforming their power sector. They have been able to reduce losses by managing state-owned power plants well and by serving their industrial customers. Industrial consumers, who were charged higher prices, cross-subsidized the losses due to theft and nonpayment of tariffs by farmers.[94]

Second, Indian agriculture faces an acute dilemma. Subsidies to this sector, as a proportion of GDP, rose steadily from 0.43 percent in the fiscal year 1990–1 to 0.74 percent in 2005–6. Increased subsidy did not produce higher rates of agricultural growth between 1990 and 2000 (2.97%), as compared to the 1980s (3.4%).[95] The average growth rate was 2.9 percent between 2000 and 2007, with some years of negative or zero growth between 2000 and 2004.[96] This dip in the rate of growth created the prospect of a second agrarian crisis in India after the mid-1960s. Reports that subsidies were growing at the expense of public investment existed. The government launched a program of substantial investment in rural development, known as Bharat Nirman (Building India), in order to address this problem. Funds available for Bharat Nirman were raised from 18.6 billion rupees ($399.9 million) in 2006

[93] Ministry of Finance, *Economic Survey 2007/08* (New Delhi: Government of India, 2008), 214.
[94] Rahul Mukherji, "Regulation and Infrastructure Development in India," *World Bank Consultation Paper* (New Delhi: The World Bank, 2008): 16–28.
[95] S. Mahendra Dev, *Inclusive Growth in India* (New Delhi: Oxford University Press, 2008), 115.
[96] The 2000–7 figures are from The Economist Intelligence Unit, accessed through the National University of Singapore library Web site (accessed December 20, 2010). For other figures of agricultural growth, see Dev, *Inclusive Growth in India*, 28.

and 2007 to 26.6 billion rupees ($572 million) in 2007 and 2008. These funds were to be used for activities including irrigation, drinking-water supply, housing, electrification, and telephony in rural areas.[97]

The growth of the agricultural sector at an annual average rate of less than 3 percent, when the economy is growing at a rate that is considerably in excess of 6 percent, has had major consequences for employment opportunities for the vast majority of Indians living in rural areas. Sociological accounts suggest that agrarian distress is pushing people out of rural areas.[98] Employment statistics for the two periods 1993–4 to 1999–2000 and 1999–2000 to 2004–5 reveal that the distress caused has been less than the low levels of agricultural growth would have predicted. Although agricultural wage employment has declined during this period, rural nonagricultural employment has grown fairly substantially.[99] People working in cities send back money to their villages and commute to cities in order to earn a livelihood.[100]

Problems of agrarian growth and distress have been accompanied with the incidence of suicides committed by farmers. Several instances of farmers' suicides in states such as Andhra Pradesh, Maharashtra, Madhya Pradesh, Chhattisgarh, and Karnataka have been reported in the media.[101] Growing scholarly evidence shows that such suicides occur largely due to a movement from subsistence to commercial agriculture.

---

[97] Dev, *Inclusive Growth in India*, 50–3.

[98] Dipankar Gupta, *The Caged Phoenix: Can India Fly?* (New Delhi: Penguin Books, 2009), 84–111.

[99] Dev, *Inclusive Growth in India*, 181.

[100] On city migrants enriching the villages, see Chandra Bhan Prasad, "Markets and Manu," *CASI Working Paper Series*, Number 08–01 (Philadelphia: University of Pennsylvania, 2008): 24–8; Goran Djurfeldt, Venkatesh Athreya, N. Jayakumar, Staffan Lindberg, A. Rajagopal, and R. Vidyasagar, "Agrarian Change and Social Mobility in Tamil Nadu," *Economic and Political Weekly* 43:45 (November 8, 2008): 52–60; Gupta, *The Caged Phoenix: Can India Fly?* 91–111.

[101] See "The Largest Wave of Suicides in History," http://www.counterpunch.org/sainath02122009.html (accessed August 3, 2010).

Commercial agriculture can be risky in the absence of social safety nets. Farmers are often lured by the prospect of profit and make investments without understanding the risks involved. A good crop can be misleading. When farmers get into risky ventures and become dependent on moneylenders but cannot pay back their loans due to a bad crop, pride rather than abject poverty takes a life. Farmers' suicides in India generally occur among those engaged in commercial farming – it is not commonplace among marginal farmers.[102]

Third, the Mahatma Gandhi National Rural Employment Guarantee Act (MGNREGA, 2005) has been hailed as a significant poverty-alleviation measure in India. It was a timely measure when the prospect of a drought loomed large in 2009. The government assured one hundred days of employment at the rate of 60 rupees ($1.29) per day. The poor engage in the production of durable public goods that are aimed at water conservation, drought proofing, expanding irrigation, and land development. This is a firm financial commitment that, unlike previous antipoverty programs, has been legislated. The MGNREGA Web site reports the progress of this program in all the districts in the country.[103] This has ensured greater transparency and accountability than was the case in the past.

To ensure that the commitments of programs such as the MGNREGA are actually met, social activists can invoke the Right to Information (RTI) Act. It is a powerful weapon in the hands of the citizen for catching corruption within the government. The act is largely the result of the struggles of the Organization for the Empowerment of Workers and Peasants (Mazdoor Kisan Shakti Sangathan, or MKSS), led by the Ramon Magsaysay award winner and social activist

---

[102] On farmer suicides, see D. Narasimha Reddy and Srijit Misra, "Agriculture in the Reforms Regime," in *Agrarian Crisis in India*, ed. D. Narasimha Reddy and Srijit Misra (New Delhi: Oxford University Press, 2009), 3–43; V. M. Rao, "Farmers' Distress in a Modernizing Agriculture," in Reddy and Misra, *Agrarian Crisis in India*, 109–25.

[103] See "The Mahatma Gandhi National Rural Employment Guarantee Act 2005," http://nrega.nic.in (accessed December 29, 2010).

Aruna Roy. MKSS pioneered the process of social audit of government policies in the 1990s when the Official Secrets Act protected government information on a host of subjects. The RTI was first passed in 2000 and amended in 2005. The 2005 amendment is a powerful legal instrument that seeks to give all Indian citizens access to information that is available to legislators.[104]

What are the results of the MGNREGA as an employ-ment-generation scheme? MGNREGA has generated about forty-seven person days per household as of December 2009.[105] Rajasthan and Andhra Pradesh are the two states that have generated the largest number of days of work. Minimum wages have increased in states such as Maharashtra, Uttar Pradesh, Bihar, Karnataka, West Bengal, Rajasthan, Madhya Pradesh, Himachal Pradesh, Nagaland, Jammu and Kashmir, and Chhattisgarh.[106] Together, scheduled castes and tribes par-ticipated in about 55 percent of the employment-generating activities at the all-India level. Women did about 48 percent of the work undertaken by MGNREGA.[107] The MGNREGA

---

[104] Aruna Roy, Nikhil Dey, and Suchi Pandey, "The Right to Information Act 2005: A Social Development Perspective," in *India: Social Develop-ment Report: 2008*, ed. Hari Mohan Mathur (New Delhi: Council for Social Development and Oxford University Press, 2008), 205–20.

[105] *Person days* refer to the number of days of employment generated by MGNREGA per household.

[106] Ministry of Rural Development, *Mahatma Gandhi National Rural Employment Guarantee Act 2005: Report to the People 2nd Feb. 2006–2nd Feb. 2010* (New Delhi: Government of India, 2010), 12, 23, 30–1. See also, "The Mahatma Gandhi National Rural Employment Guarantee Act 2005."

[107] "The Mahatma Gandhi National Rural Employment Guarantee Act 2005"; Ashok K. Pankaj, "The National Rural Employment Guarantee Act," in Mathur, *India: Social Development Report 2008*, 221–50; Jean Dreze, "Employment Guarantee and the Right to Work," in Jayal and Mehta, *The Oxford Companion to Politics in India*, 510–18; "One Rupee a Day for NREGA Labourers in Tonk," http://www.ndtv.com/news/videos/video_player.php?id=160042 (accessed December 29, 2010); P. Sainath, "NREGS: Not Caste in Stone," *The Hindu*, September 14, 2009, http://www.thehindu.com/2009/09/14/stories/2009091454990900.htm (accessed December 29, 2010).

program is not without its problems though, and corruption and leakages of funds are a matter of serious concern.[108]

Fourth, India has a food surplus but suffers from a rather poor record in nutrition. Studies reveal that 43 percent of Indian children suffered from malnutrition in 2005 and 2006. According to one estimate, the proportion of malnourished children may be higher in India than in Ethiopia.[109] The country's public-distribution system suffers from leakages and corruption. Many poor people are not included, and those that are not suffering from acute poverty are able to grab resources meant for the poor.[110] However, the Left parties in Kerala and the Dravida Munnetra Kazhagam (DMK) and the All India Anna DMK Party (AIADMK) in Tamil Nadu have played a significant role in guaranteeing food for the poor.[111] States such as Kerala, Tamil Nadu, and Himachal Pradesh have built successful public-distribution systems and enjoy a reasonable amount of food security, whereas Bihar, Uttar Pradesh, West Bengal, and Madhya Pradesh have fared poorly.[112]

[108] Raghbendra Jha, Sambit Bhattacharya, and Raghav Gaiha, "Timing of Capture of Anti-Poverty Programs," *ASARC Working Paper 2009/16* (Canberra, Australia: South Asia Research Centre, Australian National University, 2009): 1–9; "The Mahatma Gandhi National Rural Employment Guarantee Act 2005."

[109] Michael Walton, "The Political Economy of India's Malnutrition Puzzle," *IDS Bulletin* 40:4 (July 2009): 16–24.

[110] Ritika Khera, "Access to the Targeted Public Distribution System: A Case Study of Rajasthan," *Economic and Political Weekly* 44:29 (November 1, 2008): 51–6; Jos Mooij, "Food and Power in Bihar and Jharkhand," *Economic and Political Weekly* 36:34 (August 25, 2001): 3289–95, 3297–9.

[111] On interstate variation in the success of distribution of food to the poor, see Dev, *Inclusive Growth in India*, 101–31; A. K. Venkatsubramanian, "The Political Economy of the Public Distribution System in Tamil Nadu," in *Reinventing Public Service Delivery in India*, ed. Vikram K. Chand (Washington, DC, and New Delhi: The World Bank and Sage Publications), 266–93; V. K. Ramachandran, "On Kerala's Development Alternatives," in *Indian Development*, ed. Jean Dreze and Amartya Sen (New Delhi: Oxford University Press, 1996), 237–50.

[112] On interstate variation in the success of distribution of food to the poor, see Dev, *Inclusive Growth in India*, 101–31; Venkatsubramanian,

Fifth, India's record in promoting literacy is dismal compared with that of China and many other developing countries. The literacy rate for those aged between fifteen and twenty-four years in the country was 80 percent in 2005 and 2006, whereas the figure for China was 99 percent. India's story of promoting primary education has been one of dismal neglect since independence. The education sector has received only fitful attention.[113] In 1993, India's Supreme Court linked the right to literacy to the right to a decent livelihood. In 2001 and 2002 the Sarva Shiksha Abhiyan (Education for All Program) was launched and expenditure on primary education rose from 0.37 percent of India's GDP in 1950 to 1.04 percent in 1975. In 2005, the figure rose to 1.57 percent of the country's GDP. The Right to Education Bill was passed in India in August 2009, with the promise of substantial resources dedicated to free and compulsory education in India.[114] However, a significant challenge for the promotion of primary education is the prevalence of low-quality government schools that are burdened with some of the highest rates of teacher absenteeism in the world. This has resulted in the mushrooming of low-quality, cheap, private schools that serve the lower middle class and the poor. Government schools are still the only option for the children of the poorest of the poor. The substandard quality of such schools is likely to lead to a growing disparity in access to education between the children of the poor and those who can afford to send their children to better private schools.[115]

"The Political Economy of the Public Distribution System in Tamil Nadu," 266–93; Ramachandran, "On Kerala's Development Alternatives," 237–50.

[113] Figures are from the World Development Indicators, The World Bank, accessed through the National University of Singapore library Web site.

[114] Tilak, "Universalizing Elementary Education," 60–3.

[115] Ibid., 50–2; Nazmul Chaudhury, Jeffrey Hammer, Michael Kramer, Karthik Muralidharan, and F. Halsey Rogers, "Missing in Action: Teacher and Health Worker Absence in Developing Countries," *Journal of Economic Perspectives* 20:1 (Winter 2006): 101–7; Lant Pritchett and

Apart from the varying quality of primary education across states, there is considerable variation in literacy rates in India. For example, in 2001 Kerala's adult literacy rate was more than 90 percent. A historical process that involved considerable efforts on the part of Christian missionaries, the Maharaja of Travancore, and various minority groups since the early twentieth century contributed to this outcome. Non-Brahmin education was widespread in Kerala even before the advent of the British.[116] States such as Rajasthan, Madhya Pradesh, and Himachal Pradesh, which all had a substantial illiterate population at the time of independence in 1947, have succeeded in raising their literacy rates. Rajasthan is one of the few states that have a school in every village.[117] Madhya Pradesh's experiment of empowering the local village government to increase its accountability has successfully reduced teacher absenteeism in the state to one of the lowest levels in the country.[118] Evidence exists to suggest that the surge in literacy has had a positive impact on the quality of democracy in India.[119]

Sixth, the proportion of people living below the poverty line in India has declined more sharply during the postreform period after 1991 as compared to the prereform era. People debate about the extent of this decline; the debate is mostly about methodology. The fiftieth round of the National Sample

Rinku Murgai, "Teacher Compensation," *India Policy Forum 2006/07* (Washington, DC, and New Delhi: Brookings Institution and Sage Publications, 2007), 123–78.

[116] On the origins of Kerala's rise in literacy rates see Ramachandran, "On Kerala's Development Achievements," 255–74; Weiner, *The Child and the State in India*, 175–7.

[117] Prema Clarke and Jyotsna Jha, "Rajasthan's Experience in Improving Service Delivery in Education," in Chand, *Reinventing Public Service Delivery in India*, 225–65.

[118] *Reforming Public Services in India* (Washington, DC: The World Bank, 2006), 46–52.

[119] Anirudh Krishna, "Poverty and Democratic Participation Reconsidered," *Comparative Politics* 38:4 (July 2006): 439–58; Anirudh Krishna, "Politics in the Middle: Mediating Relationships between the Citizen and the State in Rural North India," in Kitschelt and Wilkinson, *Patrons, Clients and Policies*, 149–58.

Survey (1993) had relied on a questionnaire that was different from the one used in the fifty-fifth round (1999). Angus
Deaton and Jean Dreze have sought to resolve this problem by
analyzing a common basket of goods used to assess consumption levels during both these rounds. A reasonable assessment
would be to infer that the head-count ratio, or the number of
people living below the poverty line, decreased from 36 percent in 1993 to 26.1 percent in 1999 and 2000.[120]

The decline in the head-count ratio notwithstanding, India
continues to be home to the largest number of absolutely
poor people in the world. The bulk of the poor live in large,
populous heartland states, such as Bihar, Madhya Pradesh, and
Uttar Pradesh. Punjab and Haryana, the two states that have
benefited the most from the green revolution, enjoy the lowest head-count ratio in the country. Kerala, which is not a rich
state, has reduced its absolute poverty through redistributive
policies.[121]

Finally, the postreform period has witnessed a growing
gap in the rates of growth between the country's richest and
poorest states. States became more directly involved with the
task of attracting investment after industrial licensing was
abolished in 1991. Federal funds for developing poor states
also declined after 1991. Well-governed states that provided
the best investment opportunity for investors attracted investments and grew at a faster pace in this new regime. This
change in the investment regime helped entrepreneurial states
such as Maharashtra and Gujarat to grow rapidly, while the
poorer ones, including Bihar, Uttar Pradesh, and Orissa, have
lagged far behind. The gap between the richest and poorest states has grown quite substantially since the 1980s. At
this rate, growing disparities may make the richer parts of

---

[120] On the poverty debate, see Angus Deaton and Jean Dreze, "Poverty and
Inequality in India," in *Globalization and Politics in India*, ed. Baldev R.
Nayar (New Delhi: Oxford University Press, 2007), 408–57; Panagariya,
India: The Emerging Giant, 129–56.

[121] Panda, "Agriculture and Poverty Reduction," 111–27.

India resemble Singapore, while its poorer ones could begin
to mirror sub-Saharan Africa.[122]

Economic Change in India

This story of the Indian economy casts light on the gradual
process of economic change in a democratic polity. India's
tryst with development does not resemble the rapid economic
transformation in more authoritarian political settings in Asia.
First, how did politics in a democracy produce a shift from a
high degree of state control, directed toward self-reliant industrial development, to an economic regime that emphasized
the private sector, trade promotion, and accelerated growth?
Second, why did economic policies that emphasized capital-
intensive industrialization at the cost of agricultural development begin to lay a greater emphasis on food security and the
interests of farmers? Third, what explains the growing importance of the right to work and education, as well as the spurt
in the social-sector expenditure after 2004?

A shift from state-driven economic self-reliance to regulated private-sector promotion and competitiveness poses a
challenge for those who argued that the interests of the dominant coalition of industrialists, big farmers, and the bureaucracy were locked in a manner that would make a change
in the policy paradigm rather difficult in the 1980s.[123] We

---

[122] Lloyd I. Rudolph and Susanne H. Rudolph, "Iconization and
Chandrababu: Sharing Sovereignty in India's Federal Market Economy,"
in Mukherji, *India's Economic Transition*, 231–64; Montek S. Ahluwalia,
"State-Level Performance under Economic Reforms," in *Economic
Policy Reforms and the Indian Economy*, ed. Anne O. Krueger (New
Delhi: Oxford University Press, 2002), 91–122; B. B. Bhattacharya
and S. Sakthivel, in Nayar, "Regional Growth and Disparity in India,"
408–57.

[123] Economic change would be difficult according to some accounts
because the status quo reflected the balance of class forces; e.g., see
Bardhan, *The Political Economy of Development in India*. Others have
argued that economic reform could only occur stealthily in India

find that gradual economic deregulation during the 1980s prepared the ground for a major shift in policy after the 1991 balance-of-payments crisis. During the course of 1991, a substantial part of the technocracy and policy elite became convinced about the economic benefits of change arising from economic deregulation and the promotion of competitiveness than was the case in 1966 when India faced a similar crisis. They were convinced that economic self-reliance was not the optimal development path in the context of the rising demands of a highly mobilized populace. Reforming technocrats treated the 1991 balance-of-payments crisis and India's consequent dependence on the IMF as an opportunity to deal with powerful interest groups that favored the status quo. Changes in industrial and trade policy between 1991 and 1993 produced the most substantial shift toward promoting India's private sector, competitiveness, and trade.

Our post-1991 cases also suggest that political and technocratic support for change during various financial crises that hit specific sectors were essential for significant economic reform in India. First, regulation in the telecommunications sector could only be consolidated in 2000 when private companies and government-owned financial organizations became financially unviable as a result of predatory regulations that favored government-owned companies. Prime Minister Vajpayee's leadership was vital for dealing with a DOT that was averse to private-sector participation. Second, reforms leading to greater transparency in India's stock-market transactions needed to wait until the 2003 stock-market crisis. The Ministry of Finance was convinced that the collapse of the stock market would hurt the capacity of Indian industry to

(e.g., Jenkins, *Democratic Politics and Economic Reform in India*), or because the Left parties acquiesced to the economic reforms of the Congress Party in 1991 that involved elite constituencies, in order to combat a more serious enemy – Hindu nationalism (e.g., see Ashutosh Varshney, "Mass Politics or Elite Politics?" in Mukherji, *India's Economic Transition*, 145–69). These accounts emphasize the status quo bias and the sheer difficulty in realizing economic change in India.

mobilize financial resources. This conviction was the primary reason for coercing the powerful brokers of the BSE to accept higher standards of transparency in dealing with settlements. Initiatives emanating from society were no less significant than the governance efforts of the state in this story of development. A resilient society often compensated for the state's failure. For example, entrepreneurs responded brilliantly to changes in industrial regulation despite substantial infrastructural and regulatory bottlenecks; legislation and investments for promoting literacy often succeeded when supported by church and nongovernmental organizations like the MKSS (Rajasthan); and pressures from below were essential for the promotion of employment-guarantee and food-security programs. Poor governance, which manifests itself when teachers and health workers are often absent and when the food and work meant for the poor are siphoned for richer sections of the society, are service-delivery failures that hurt citizen welfare.

Significant challenges relating to investment keep India from realizing its growth potential. First, areas of physical infrastructure such as power, roads, airports, and ports are in need of serious reform. Efficient infrastructure provisions are essential to ensure India's competitiveness and economic growth in the future.[124] Second, although industrial licensing was largely abolished and foreign-investment norms made more liberal in 1991, there are still a large number of state-level clearances that pose a challenge for foreign and domestic investors in the country.[125]

India's inability to make its economic growth process more inclusive poses the most significant challenge for development. Can public investment in agriculture be redirected to

---

[124] Rahul Mukherji, "Regulation and Infrastructure Development in India: A Comparison of Telecommunications, Ports and Power," in *Public Service Delivery in India*, ed. Vikram Chand (New Delhi: Oxford University Press, 2010), 178–225.

[125] Nuashad Forbes, "Doing Business in India," in Krueger, *Economic Policy and Reforms in the Indian Economy*, 129–68.

ensure that it benefits the poorer farmers? Can rich farmers be forced to pay for power consumption? How can social-security benefits be devised for farmers so that risky investments do not result in suicides? How can corruption in employment-guarantee and food-distribution schemes be checked in order to accelerate the process of lifting the poor from despicable human conditions? How can teachers and health workers be persuaded to attend their work sites in order to do their jobs?

The poor rural voter won greater respect from the government after the 2004 general elections. Economic reforms in a democratic polity have been characterized with increasing levels of political awareness among the poor, a phenomenon that is described in Chapter 4. There has been a substantial rise in the commitment of resources for the social sector after 2004, with India embarking on the path to developing a welfare state in which the right to work and the right to become literate have become enshrined in law, and significant legislation on the right to food is also on the anvil. It can be conjectured that the strategy of securing welfare for the poor after the 2004 election victory of the United Progressive Alliance, led by the Congress Party, was rewarded by the people in a more convincing electoral verdict in favor of the Congress Party in 2009. Democratic participation may be playing a silent role in making India's economic growth more inclusive.[126]

India's experience with economic development suggests that, although economic growth is necessary, it is not sufficient for engendering human welfare. Incumbents in the public and private sectors and rent-seeking officials fiercely oppose changes that would promote greater competition and economic growth. Welfare is increasingly inspired by political

---

[126] The experience of democracy and the market has produced the welfare state in the West. See Karl Polanyi, *The Great Transformation: The Political and Economic Origins of Our Times* (Boston: Beacon Press, 1957), 223–58.

mobilization, which is driven by the power of the ballot box. Development is a social process that is in need of a state that can marry its citizens' concerns with the requirements of economic growth. This is a challenge and an opportunity at a time when the power and creativity of Indian entrepreneurs have to contend with demands from a society in which larger numbers of people are demanding the rights that the framers of the Indian constitution had sought to grant the country's citizens.

4

Political Mobilization in India

On May 17, 2009, India concluded its fifteenth general election. This proved to be the largest democratic electoral exercise in the country's and the world's history. The country had an eligible electorate of 714 million voters and 58 percent chose to exercise their right of adult franchise.[1] The results of the election confounded the most astute political analysts and observers, all of whom failed to predict its outcomes. The Indian National Congress, which many had expected to fare poorly, performed extraordinarily well, winning as many as 206 seats in a 543-seat parliament. The grand hopes that many political pundits, especially those with left-wing political proclivities, had reposed in the so-called Third Front, a conglomeration of political parties coalesced around the lower-caste oriented Bahujan Samaj Party (BSP), proved to be completely ill-considered. The BSP under the tutelage of Kumari Mayawati, a *dalit* ("untouchable") politician (and the chief minister) from the populous and socially retrograde state of Uttar Pradesh, failed to dramatically increase its standing in the Lok Sabha, or the House of the People, winning a mere

---

[1] Christophe Jaffrelot and Giles Verniers, "India's 2009 Elections: The Resilience of Regionalism and Ethnicity," *South Asia Multidisciplinary Academic Journal* 3 (2009): 1. See *South Asia Multidisciplinary Academic Journal*, http://samaj.revues.org/index2787.html (accessed December 29, 2010).

twenty seats out of a possible eighty. The Indian National Congress, which had once dominated the politics of the state, managed to obtain twenty-one seats, relegating the hypernationalist Bharatiya Janata Party (BJP) to ten seats. What explained the abject failure of Indian and foreign political analysts to accurately predict the outcome of this election? In considerable measure, the answer must be sought in the dramatic political mobilization that has taken place in India since the early 1980s. India's poor and dispossessed may wield little or no material clout, but they have come to fully understand the significance of the power of the ballot.[2] In retrospect, a number of political pundits explained Mayawati's rout in her home state in terms of her colossal failure to improve the socioeconomic conditions of the vast majority of its populace. During her tenure as the chief minister, she has been known more for the construction of various edifices extolling the virtues and contributions of India's great untouchable leader and one of the key drafters of the Indian constitution, Bhimrao Ambedkar, than anything else.[3]

The results of the election were, no doubt, laudable from the standpoint of the extension of democratic franchise. However, the "silent revolution" – to use Christophe Jaffrelot's term – that it represents is taking place in a disturbing political context. Political institutions have witnessed a remarkable breakdown in significant parts of northern India since the late 1970s.[4] Consequently, although a significant segment of the country may now have a more informed and mobilized electorate, the capacity and efficacy of institutions to

[2] For the best discussion of the subject, see Christophe Jaffrelot, *India's Silent Revolution: The Rise of Lower Castes in North India* (New York: Columbia University Press, 2002).

[3] On her early career and rise in Uttar Pradesh's politics, see Paranjoy Guha Thakurta and Shankar Raghuraman, *Divided We Stand: India in a Time of Coalitions* (New Delhi: Sage Publications, 2007).

[4] For an early discussion, see James Manor, "Anomie in Indian Politics: Origins and Wider Impact," *Economic and Political Weekly* 18:19 (May 21, 1983): 725–34.

meet the greater social expectations and political demands are sorely wanting.

This problem, of expanding demands for political participation and anemic political institutions, had been identified as early as 1968 in the work of the noted American political scientist Samuel Huntington.[5] In this work, Huntington accurately identified the dangers of political instability that could ensue if political mobilization exceeded the capacity of existing institutions to cope and channel concomitant demands. Fortunately, when this form of political mobilization swept through southern India during the 1960s, thereby overturning an extant social order and enfranchising a new generation of lower castes, India's political institutions were remarkably robust. Consequently, they proved to be quite resilient in responding to and coping with the demands that ensued as a consequence of political awakening and mobilization.[6] How India's political institutions, which have witnessed much decay during the past several decades, respond to the new set of challenges remains an open question.

The Origins of Political Mobilization

How did this form of dramatic political mobilization ensue in India throughout the last three decades? What have been its principal manifestations? How has such mobilization altered the texture and context of Indian politics? This chapter will try to trace the origins of this dramatic pace of political mobilization, discuss its emergence, and then analyze its consequences for India's contemporary politics.

The roots of political mobilization in northern and southern India can be traced to the growing political consciousness of

---

[5] Samuel Huntington, *Political Order in Changing Societies* (New Haven, CT: Yale University Press, 1968).

[6] For a discussion, see Robert L. Hardgrave Jr., *The Nadars of Tamilnad: The Political Culture of a Community in Change* (Berkeley: University of California Press, 1969).

lower-caste groups that include backward-caste groups and the lowest stratum in the social hierarchy – the scheduled castes also known as the *dalits*. The standing of backward castes in India's complex social hierarchy can be located between the socially privileged upper castes and the "untouchables" or *dalits*. The backward-caste groups became the principal beneficiaries of land reforms, a key factor in their subsequent political mobilization.[7] Despite the Congress Party's professed and real commitment to social diversity,[8] for all practical purposes, in the years after India's independence it was still a high-caste-dominated organization.[9]

The backward castes had opposed Prime Minister Nehru's (1947–64) emphasis on investments in heavy industrialization in the Second Five-Year Plan (1956–61) because these beneficiaries of land reforms found that pricing and investment policies discriminated against the agricultural sector. Nehru had hoped that organizational changes alone, such as the redistribution of land from rich landlords to tenants and the collectivization of agriculture, would lead to substantial increases in agricultural productivity. Land reforms were partially successful during the mid-1950s. They benefited the larger tenants who belonged to the backward-caste groups and freed up fourteen million acres of land for about twenty million tenants. The abolition of tenant intermediaries during the mid-1950s increased the proportion of owner cultivators in India from 40 percent to 75 percent.[10] The clarion call at that time was

---

[7] On the benefits that accrued to backward-caste groups as a result of land reforms, see Lloyd I. Rudolph and Susanne H. Rudolph, *In Pursuit of Lakshmi: The Political Economy of the Indian State* (Chicago: University of Chicago Press, 1987), 333–92; Francine Frankel, *India's Green Revolution: Economic Gains and Political Costs* (Princeton, NJ: Princeton University Press, 1971).

[8] See, e.g., Rajni Kothari, "The Congress System in India," *Asian Survey* 4:12 (1964): 1161–73.

[9] Jaffrelot, *India's Silent Revolution*.

[10] Rudolph and Rudolph, *In Pursuit of Lakshmi*, 314–15; Ashutosh Varshney, *Democracy, Development and the Countryside* (New York: Cambridge University Press, 1998), 31–47.

"land to the tiller."[11] The benefits for the large tenants were spread over states such as Uttar Pradesh, Rajasthan, Gujarat, Assam, Bihar, West Bengal, Orissa, and Hyderabad.[12]

The partial success of land reforms converted tenants into landowners and created a class of numerous "bullock capitalists," who owned between 2.5 and 15 acres of land. The backward-caste-dominated class of bullock capitalists opposed the Nehruvian plan in no uncertain terms by demanding better prices and greater investment in agriculture.[13] Charan Singh, a farmers' leader from the heartland and populous state of Uttar Pradesh, had championed the cause of land reforms during the early 1950s as the revenue minister of Uttar Pradesh and had successfully opposed the ruling Congress Party's resolve to initiate cooperative farming in 1959. He had opposed the view within the Congress that rural and agrarian sectors should serve the ends of urbanization and industrialization and had demanded greater attention to rural India. Singh had resigned from the Congress Party, formed his own Bharatiya Lok Dal, and earned the distinction of becoming the first non–Congress Party chief minister of Uttar Pradesh in 1967.[14]

In the state-level and national elections that occurred between 1967 and 1969, parties representing the backward castes such as the Dravida Munnetra Kazhagam (DMK) in Tamil Nadu; the Socialist Party and the Praja Socialist Party in Bihar and Uttar Pradesh; and the Bharatiya Kranti Dal in Uttar Pradesh made inroads into the Congress Party's dominance. The fourth general election in 1967 was the first time that the Congress Party won less than 70 percent of the seats

[11] Ronald J. Herring, *Land to the Tiller* (New Haven, CT: Yale University Press, 1983).

[12] Shalendra D. Sharma, *Development and Democracy in India* (Boulder, CO: Lynne Reinner, 1999), 112.

[13] Rudolph and Rudolph, *In Pursuit of Lakshmi*, 335–46.

[14] On Charan Singh, see Paul Brass, "Chaudhuri Charan Singh: An Indian Political Life," *Economic and Political Weekly* 28:39 (September 25, 1993): 2087–90; Jaffrelot, *India's Silent Revolution*, 279–311.

in India's Parliament (Lok Sabha). The anti–Congress Party backward-caste vote proved a significant challenge for the Congress Party. At the state level, the Congress Party lost power in eight assemblies between 1967 and 1969: Bihar, Kerala, Madras, Orissa, Punjab, Rajasthan, Uttar Pradesh, and West Bengal.[15]

Ram Manohar Lohia, an influential socialist leader of the backward castes from Bihar, was one of the architects of political opposition to the Congress Party in northern India in 1967. He had begun his career as a socialist and a rebel within the Congress Party and had supported reservations in government jobs for the backward-caste groups. In 1967, his Samyukta Socialist Party, the Communist Party of India, the Communist Party of India (Marxist), and the right-wing Jana Sangh came together to topple the Congress Party government in Bihar. The new chief minister of Bihar, Karpoori Thakur, belonged to a caste that had traditionally been barbers.[16]

Backward-caste mobilization contributed significantly to the Congress Party's electoral setback in southern India after 1967. The DMK Party, an anti-Brahmin party with a radical ideology of uplift of the backward castes, also emerged triumphant in the southern state of Tamil Nadu in 1967.[17] The state of Tamil Nadu emerged as the one state in which the Congress Party could never win an election after 1967. The DMK Party reigned supreme until the mid-1970s. The party was challenged by the Anna Dravida

---

[15] Rajni Kothari, *Politics in India* (New Delhi: Orient BlackSwan, 2009): 177–90; Vernon Hewitt, *Political Mobilization and Democracy in India* (London: Routledge, 2009), 77–85.

[16] Frankel, "The Middle Classes and Castes in India's Politics," in *India's Democracy*, ed. Atul Kohli (Princeton, NJ: Princeton University Press, 1971), 249–50; Christophe Jaffrelot, "The Rise of Backward Classes in the Hindi Belt," *The Journal of Asian Studies* 59:1 (February 2000): 90; Lewis P. Fickett Jr., "The Major Socialist Parties of India in the 1967 Election," *Asian Survey* 8:6 (June 1968): 489–98.

[17] Narendra Subramanian, *Ethnicity and Populist Mobilization: Political Parties, Citizenship and Democracy in South India* (New Delhi: Oxford University Press, 1999).

Munnetra Kazhagam Party (ADMK) led by the charismatic
M. G. Ramachandran. Ramachandran, popularly known as
MGR, was a leading film actor who had played the roles of a
savior of the dispossessed. His numerous fan clubs praised his
virtues as a hero and philanthropist. He was effectively able
to use the medium of film as a tool to mobilize voters in a
state in which literacy rates were quite dismal at that time.
MGR left the Congress Party to join the DMK in 1953. His
popularity within the DMK and the unease of the old guard
within the party led him to form a separate All India Anna
DMK Party (AIADMK) in 1972. One of the best scholarly
accounts of political mobilization in Tamil Nadu suggests that
the AIADMK Party succeeded by moderating the demands
emanating from Tamil subnationalism.[18] It attracted the *dalits*
or lowest castes in the social-order hierarchy as well as the
upper castes, while holding on to the backward-caste vote.

The political mobilization of backward-caste groups could
not be accommodated within the existing structure and
organization of the Congress Party. The plebiscitary politics
that Prime Minister Indira Gandhi (1966–75, 1980–4) had
embarked upon after 1968 in an attempt to bolster her own
political fortunes and to undercut her opponents within the
Congress Party contributed to the political mobilization of
the backward-caste groups. She was appointed prime minister
in 1966 at a time when backward-caste and proagricultural
interests were being mobilized. This was also a time when
India was faced with multiple crises including poor mon-
soons, concomitant food shortages, and a foreign-exchange
shortage.[19] Moreover, she was a young prime minister who

---

[18] Ibid., 247–310; Narendra Subramanian, "Identity Politics and Social
Pluralism: Political Sociology and Political Change in Tamil Nadu,"
in *Decentering the Indian Nation*, ed. Andrew Wyatt and John Zavos
(London: Frank Cass, 2003), 125–39.

[19] On the management of the foreign-exchange crisis see Rahul
Mukherji, "India's Aborted Liberalization – 1966," *Pacific Affairs* 73:3
(2000): 375–92; Francine R. Frankel, *India's Political Economy: 1947–
2004* (New Delhi: Oxford University Press, 2005), 283–308.

was being used by senior party officials to fill that high position until they settled their own differences.[20] Indira Gandhi could have followed a more accommodative political strategy, which might have granted the backward castes a more substantial role within the party. However, she chose not to do so.[21]

Instead, she undermined democratic procedures within the Congress Party and the government. Her decision to take on the political notables within her party and assert her dominance and that of her allies within it has been discussed at length elsewhere. Suffice it to say that she had successfully split the party in 1969 and then chose to take it in a decidedly populist direction.[22] In a 1971 election, she had won by a landslide majority by relying on a slogan of "*garibi hatao,*" or "abolish poverty." With a secure parliamentary majority she had moved the country in a decidedly leftward direction, abolishing the "privy purses" (state subventions to the former princely rulers in India), nationalizing banks, and expanding India's public sector. All these populist gestures, though not entirely sound from the perspective of rational economic policy making, nevertheless enabled her to transcend party politics and reach out directly to significant segments of India's electorate.

Simultaneously, as a number of commentators have discussed at length, she had aggrandized political power at the national level, contributed to the organizational decline of the Congress Party, and sought to subvert key political institutions, most notably the Indian Supreme Court, an entity that had attempted to hobble her propensity to expand executive power.[23] The organizational decline of the Congress Party had significant consequences for Indian politics. Among other

[20] Frankel, *India's Political Economy*, 288–92.

[21] Atul Kohli, "Political Change in a Democratic Developing Country," in *Democracy in India*, ed. Niraja G Jayal (New Delhi: Oxford University Press, 2001), 140–7.

[22] See the discussion in Frankel, *India's Political Economy*, 388–433.

[23] Much of this is discussed in Paul R. Brass, *The Politics of India since Independence* (Cambridge: Cambridge University Press, 1994).

matters, it enabled other political parties, especially at the level of various states, to highlight local issues and grievances and to mobilize and tap into an electorate that no longer saw the Congress Party as the only viable choice. Ironically, the growth of possible alternatives to the Congress Party only made her even more intransigent toward these incipient political forces and led her to resort to constitutionally questionable means in order to undermine them.

Her willingness to undermine robust political and institutional norms was most strikingly on display when she faced the possibility of prosecution for a number of minor electoral offenses in 1976. In a blatant attempt to ensure her own political survival, she resorted to a declaration of a "state of emergency" to avoid prosecution and removal from political office.[24] During this state of emergency, she squelched personal rights and civil liberties, implemented a draconian birth-control program, and incarcerated much of the political opposition.[25]

Probably in an attempt to restore her political legitimacy, and because she was dependent upon the advice of a coterie of sycophantic advisers, she lifted the state of emergency in 1977 and called for national elections. An unlikely combination of political parties, including elements of the Indian right wing, represented by the Bharatiya Jana Sangh (BJS); two socialist parties; and elements of the old order of the Congress Party led by Morarji Desai, a Gandhian stalwart in the party, challenged Prime Minister Gandhi. This loose conglomeration, known as the Janata Party, contributed to her political

---

[24] For a discussion of the forces that led up to the emergency, see Henry Hart, ed., *Indira Gandhi's India: A Political System Reappraised* (Boulder, CO: Westview Press, 1986).

[25] The best assessment of the effects of the state of emergency remains Jyotirindra Das Gupta, "A Season of Caesars: Mobilization Regimes and Development Politics in Asia," *Asian Survey* 18:4 (April 1978): 315–49; also see the discussion in Francine R. Frankel, "Compulsion and Social Change: Is Authoritarianism the Solution to India's Economic Development Problems?" *World Politics* 30:2 (January 1978): 215–40.

rout in considerable part because of the population's acute resentment of the high-handedness of governmental officials at all levels during the state of emergency.[26] The Janata Party's victory in 1977 was a triumph of the backward-caste groups over the Congress Party's dominance at the national level for the first time. Charan Singh, a backward-caste leader of the farmers in northern India, was appointed deputy prime minister with the responsibility of selecting three important chief ministers in Bihar, Uttar Pradesh, and Haryana.[27]

Unfortunately, the Janata Dal quickly fell prey to internecine political squabbles based upon policy and personal differences, and the Janata phase of Indian politics came to a close in 1979 with the collapse of the regime.[28] It is widely believed that Indira Gandhi was able to stage a political comeback largely because the Janata regime, despite its sterling efforts to restore personal rights, civil liberties, and press freedoms, displayed a singular inability to formulate effective policies and govern. The Janata Party's loss in 1980 has been attributed to the inability of the backward-caste groups to maintain a stable coalition and the ability of the Congress Party to splinter the backward-caste vote.[29]

After the Second Coming of Indira Gandhi

Many of the political choices that Indira Gandhi made during the early 1980s would further undermine the quality of India's political institutions.[30] Among other matters, she

[26] A careful discussion of the political context of the state of emergency and its aftermath can be found in Hewitt, *Political Mobilization and Democracy in India*.

[27] Jaffrelot, *India's Silent Revolution*, 305–34; Arun R. Swamy, "Political Mobilization," in *The Oxford Companion to Politics in India*, ed. Niraja G. Jayal and Pratap B. Mehta (New Delhi: Oxford University Press, 2010), 268–87.

[28] Hewitt, *Political Mobilization and Democracy in India*.

[29] Frankel, "The Middle Classes and Castes in India's Politics," 256–9.

[30] For a trenchant discussion, see Robert L. Hardgrave Jr., *India under Pressure: Prospects for Political Stability* (Boulder, CO: Westview Press, 1984).

fecklessly utilized the powers granted to the prime minister under Article 356 of the Indian constitution to dismiss state governments. She also resorted to a number of other extra-constitutional tactics in order to undermine the emergence of political alternatives in a number of states ranging from Assam to Punjab and Kashmir. Her political machinations had tragic and highly corrosive consequences for Indian federalism, the judiciary, the Indian National Congress, and, concomitantly, the country's political order.[31]

The southern state of Andhra Pradesh witnessed the emergence of a substantial rival party to the Congress Party. This can be mostly attributed to the Congress Party's centralizing propensities at the cost of paying attention to local concerns. The Telegu Desam Party (TDP) in Andhra Pradesh led by the charismatic film actor N. T. Rama Rao outflanked the Congress Party in 1983. It is widely believed that Prime Minister Gandhi's attempts to directly reach the *dalits* while bypassing the regional party organization were to blame for the birth of the new party, which would rule the state from 1983 to 2004. She neglected the concerns of the Congress Party at the state level when determining important party and ministerial positions. Chief Minister P. V. Narasimha Rao, who was loyal to Prime Minister Gandhi, became very unpopular for faithfully implementing policies of the Central government that may have benefited the *dalits* but not the backward and upper castes. He had to be called back to the Central government in 1973. He was effectively opposed by the backward-caste groups. His successor Vengala Rao had to go slow with the implementation of Prime Minister Indira Gandhi's "Twenty Point Programme," which included radical land reforms that would hurt the backward-caste groups that had benefited from the first phase of land reforms and did not want to further dilute their land holdings.[32]

---

[31] On her impact on the Indian judiciary, see R. Sudarshan, "In Quest of State: Politics and Judiciary in India," *The Journal of Commonwealth and Comparative Politics* 28:1 (March 1990): 44–69.

[32] Ram Reddy, "The Politics of Accommodation: Caste, Class and Dominance in Andhra Pradesh," in *Dominance and State Power in Modern*

N. T. Rama Rao, a charismatic film actor who had played the roles of mythological incarnations of various Hindu gods, and his successor and son-in-law Chandra Babu Naidu took advantage of the popular resentment against the Central government's undue interference in the affairs of Andhra Pradesh. The backward castes that comprised 40 percent of the voters supported N. T. Rama Rao in the 1983 elections. The TDP was able to consolidate the votes that had previously gone to the non-Congress national parties that had earned the support of backward-caste groups such as the Lok Dal, the socialist parties, and the Janata Party.[33]

The organizational decline of the Congress Party; the growth of political mobilization, in large part due to Gandhi's various populist schemes and gestures; and the rise of new political parties in key states posed important challenges to her dominance of India's politics. As a consequence of the confluence of many of these factors and of her propensity for political chicanery, she contributed to a critical political crisis in the Punjab. Her involvement in the politics of the Punjab arose in large measure as a consequence of the rise of a local party, the Akali Dal, which posed a challenge to the dominance of the Congress Party in the state.[34]

Specifically, she encouraged the rise of an itinerant Sikh preacher, Sant Jarnail Singh Bhindranwale, who was opposed to the Akalis. Bhindranwale, who had a charismatic personality and promoted a very parochial view of Sikhism, quickly attracted a following among those in the Punjab whose livelihoods the green revolution had disrupted. The green revolution had brought about the transformation of the rural, agricultural

India: Decline of a Social Order, ed. Francine Frankel and M. S. A. Rao (Delhi: Oxford University Press, 1990), 282–92; Frankel, "The Middle Classes and Castes in India's Politics," 246–8.

[33] K. C. Suri, "Telegu Desam Party," in India's Political Parties, ed. Peter Ronald deSouza and E. Sridharan (New Delhi: Sage Publications, 2006), 283–7.

[34] See the excellent discussion in Katherine Frank, Indira: The Life of Indira Nehru Gandhi (London: HarperCollins, 2001).

economy of the Punjab through the introduction of disease-resistant, high-yielding seeds and agricultural technology.[35]

Very soon, Bhindranwale's tactics turned violent, and Prime Minister Gandhi realized that she had little control over him especially as he and his followers ensconced themselves in the holiest shrine of Sikhism in the Golden Temple in the city of Amritsar in the Punjab.[36] As political instability and violence in the Punjab metamorphosed into a crisis during 1984, she ordered the Indian Army to storm the temple and dislodge Bhindranwale and his followers. The military carried out an assault on the temple, in which Bhindranwale and many of his followers were killed along with a number of pilgrims. For a variety of complex reasons, which have been discussed at length elsewhere, the military operation was poorly conceived and clumsily executed.[37] The military operation alienated significant segments of the Sikh community. The military action even earned the ire of those within the community who were not supporters of the separatist movement. In a particularly tragic turn, two of Indira Gandhi's Sikh bodyguards assassinated her on October 31, 1984, as she was on her way from her residence to an interview for the British Broadcasting Corporation with the noted actor Peter Ustinov.

In the Aftermath of Indira Gandhi

Political mobilization continued apace, albeit in very different ways in the aftermath of Prime Minister Gandhi's assassination.

---

[35] Francine R. Frankel, *India's Green Revolution: Economic Gains and Political Costs* (Princeton, NJ: Princeton University Press, 1971).

[36] Mark Tully and Satish Jacob, *Amritsar: Mrs. Gandhi's Last Battle* (London: Jonathan Cape, 1986).

[37] See the detailed analysis in C. Christine Fair, "The Golden Temple: A Tale of Two Sieges," in *Treading on Hallowed Ground: Counterinsurgency Operations in Sacred Places*, ed. C. Christine Fair and Sumit Ganguly (New York: Oxford University Press, 2007); for a broader discussion of the Sikh insurgency, see Kirpal Dhillon, *Identity and Survival: Sikh Militancy in India, 1978–1993* (New Delhi: Penguin Books, 2006).

In an attempt to capitalize on the widespread sympathy for Prime Minister Gandhi in the wake of her assassination, the Congress Party chose to nominate her son, Rajiv Gandhi, as her successor. This strategy paid handsomely for the Congress Party, and it won as many as 411 seats in a 542-seat parliament. With this very substantial mandate, Rajiv Gandhi undertook a number of initiatives on a variety of possible fronts. At the outset, he sought to undo some of the significant damage of his mother's political legacies. To that end, he signed accords with local leaders in Assam and the Punjab, thereby paving the way toward a return to some semblance of political stability. His most important endeavor, however, was a dramatic attempt to modernize the Indian economy and to move it away from its hidebound, state-led model of economic growth, which had long outlived its usefulness.

Unfortunately, this effort, which had engendered significant hopes within and outside of India, for a transformation of the Indian economy, came to an abrupt halt. A number of interest groups – within and outside of the Congress Party – that stood to lose their prerogatives and privileges in a more open and competitive economy, significantly hobbled his efforts.[38] His attempts to bring about internal organizational reform within the Congress Party also met with a similar fate as he faced significant opposition from party notables; individuals whom his mother and his brother, Sanjay Gandhi, had brought in; and regional satraps, or local wielders of political power. In part his inability to bring about institutional reforms stemmed from the limits of his personal electoral popularity. As it started to wane, those who had long wielded political power within the party, and stood to lose much of their clout if his efforts at reform became effective, struck back with a vengeance.[39]

---

[38] For an astute and considered discussion of the problems that confronted Rajiv Gandhi, see Barnett Rubin, "Economic Liberalization and the Indian State," *Third World Quarterly* 7:4 (October 1985): 942–57.

[39] For a highly informative and trenchant account of Rajiv Gandhi's efforts at economic and political reforms and how they were stymied, see Atul Kohli, *Democracy and Discontent: India's Growing Crisis of Governability* (Cambridge: Cambridge University Press, 1990).

Later on, as he became embroiled in other controversies, most notably accusations about corruption involving the purchase of field artillery for the Indian Army from a Swedish firm, Bofors, his penchant for and ability to push through much-needed organizational reforms within the party simply drew to a close.

A significant area of political mobilization at a time of continuing institutional decay during the Rajiv Gandhi era was the rise of farmer's movements during the 1980s. We have already described the rise of bullock capitalists who were located somewhere between the marginal and landless farmers and the large landlords.[40] These farmers had benefited enormously from the green revolution during the early 1970s and had found greater voice in policy matters during the Janata Party regime (1977–9).[41] They had become especially vocal in the 1980s. Organizations like Bharatiya Kisan Union (Indian Farmer's Union) in North India, the Shetkari Sangathan in Maharashtra, and the Tamil Agriculturists Association demanded higher input subsidies and procurement prices for food grains. Their political tactics were extralegal and crude. They organized massive rallies, created roadblocks, and beat up electricity officials (who came to collect bills) in order to get their demands heard. They did not represent the large or the marginal farmers. Their most important support base was the bullock capitalists owning anywhere between 1.5 and 15 acres of land, who usually belonged to the backward-caste community.[42] This community created a political base

[40] Rudolph and Rudolph, *In Pursuit of Lakshmi*, 333–92.
[41] The green revolution is described in Chapter 3. This was a strategy of agricultural reform, which was based on substantial investments in agriculture from the mid-1960s.
[42] On farmer's movements in the 1980s, see Jim Bentall and Stuart Corbridge, "Demand Politics and the 'New Agrarianism' in Northwest India: The Bharatiya Kisan Union," *Transactions of the Institute of British Geographers*, New Series, 21:1 (1996): 27–48; Akhil Gupta, *Postcolonial Developments: Agriculture in the Making of Modern India* (Durham, NC: Duke University Press, 1998), 33–105; Gail Omvedt, "Farmer's Movements and the Debate on Poverty and Economic Reforms in India," in *Social Movements in India: Poverty, Power and Politics*, ed. Raka

for opposition to Rajiv Gandhi and the Congress Party during the 1980s.

V. P. Singh and the Politics of the Mandal Commission Report

Rajiv Gandhi's regime had ushered in an era of partial economic liberalization. The consequences that ensued, for good and ill, are discussed in Chapter 3. Unfortunately, his regime became ensnared in a major political scandal with allegations about bribery in the selection of the Bofors field gun for the Indian Army. This led to the resignation of Minister of Finance Vishwanath Pratap Singh and, ultimately, to his departure from the Congress Party. In the 1989 national elections, the Congress Party suffered an important electoral setback, and yet another coalition, with V. P. Singh as its leader, came to power. Shortly after assuming power in 1990, V. P. Singh, probably as a consequence of electoral calculation and political conviction, chose to implement a new affirmative-action plan based upon the findings and recommendations of a governmental commission, the Mandal Commission Report. The report had been drafted under the Janata Party regime during 1979 under the leadership of Bindeshwari Prasad Mandal, a politician from the state of Bihar.

One of the key ramifications of the implementation of the Mandal Commission Report was that it held out prospects for the entry of a host of socially disadvantaged backward-caste groups into secure government employment. Because this sweeping decision was made at a time when prospects of employment in the private sector were still limited and when the security of state employment was deemed paramount, its impact on India's lower castes cannot be underestimated. The

Ray and Mary Fainsod Katzenstien (New Delhi: Oxford University Press, 2005), 179–202; Zoya Hasan, "Transfer of Power: Politics of Mass Mobilization in UP," *Economic and Political Weekly* 36:46/47 (November 24, 2001): 4401–9.

ability to obtain a significant share of such employment and other benefits that the state can dole out had been the foci of much lower-caste mobilization.[43]

Two factors, it appears, explain Singh's embrace of this strategy. First, he recognized other political leaders in northern India had already won over middle peasants. Consequently, he sought a strategy that would appeal to and empower lower castes. Second, with his socialist leanings, he had concluded that the caste system also embodied political power. To break the stranglehold on political power it was necessary to strengthen the hands of lower castes under the rubric of "other backward castes," or OBCs.[44] As Christophe Jaffrelot has written:

> Their new unity helped the "Other Backward Castes" (OBCs) to organize themselves as an interest group outside the vertical, clientelistic Congress-like patterns. The aim was to benefit from this main asset, its massive numbers (52 percent of the Indian population), at the time of elections. Indeed, the share of the OBC MPs [members of Parliament] increased in the Hindi belt because lower-caste people became more aware of their common interests and decided to no longer vote for upper-caste candidates.[45]

Members of India's OBCs who were the principal beneficiaries of this program of affirmative action, which promised to reserve 27 percent of all government employment for them, were understandably pleased with this decision. This reservation would come on top of 22.5 percent of positions that were already reserved for the so-called scheduled castes

---

[43] For an extensive analysis of how this form of government patronage has played out in India, see Kanchan Chandra, *Why Ethnic Parties Succeed: Patronage and Ethnic Head Counts in India* (Cambridge: Cambridge University Press, 2004).

[44] For a largely sympathetic account, see Gail Omvedt, "The Anti-caste Movement and the Discourse of Power," in *Democracy in India*, ed. Niraja Gopal Jayal (New Delhi: Oxford University Press, 2001).

[45] Christophe Jaffrelot, "The Rise of Other Backward Classes in the Hindi Belt," *Journal of Asian Studies* 59:1 (February 2000): 86–108; quotation is on p. 98.

and tribes. It should be noted that regional politicians had already sought to mobilize the OBCs, initially in Maharashtra and subsequently in Uttar Pradesh. A local leader of the OBCs in Uttar Pradesh, Mulayam Singh Yadav, was able to mobilize substantial support among the intermediate castes and formed the Samajwadi Party in order to represent their interests. He initially became the chief minister in 1989, in 1993, and, finally, between 2003 and 2007.[46]

Scheduled castes, who constitute the most disadvantaged in Indian society, also mobilized for political action in the state of Uttar Pradesh. An astute leader of the scheduled castes, Kanshi Ram, who had personally experienced discrimination, had initially formed the Backward and Minority Communities Employees Federation (BAMCEF) in order to enhance the political clout of the ethnic communities that it represented. Subsequently, he had formed the BSP in 1984, seeking to amalgamate the interests of a host of marginalized social groups. The scheduled caste groups had been the traditional supporters of the Congress Party. Over time, they realized that they had won only a token representation in the party, in which critical government and party positions were occupied by the upper-caste groups. This "representational blockage" led them to mobilize separately from the Congress Party in India's most populous state of Uttar Pradesh. In 2007, the BSP posed a successful challenge to Mulayam Singh Yadav, effectively ousting him from office. The backward-caste groups, being more numerous than the scheduled-caste population, have had to adopt

---

[46] Ibid. Two states where OBC or backward-caste mobilizations have not produced greater representation in the state legislatures or ministries include the Left-ruled states of Kerala and West Bengal. See Stephanie Tawa Lama-Rewal, "The Resilient Bhadralok: A Profile of the West Bengal MLAs," in *The Rise of the Plebians*, ed. Christophe Jaffrelot and Sanjay Kumar (New Delhi: Routledge, 2009), 361–92; G. Gopa Kumar, "Socio-economic Background of Legislators in Kerala," in Jaffrelot and Kumar, *The Rise of the Plebians*, 393–406. This is despite the fact that they have had non–Congress Party governments since the late 1960s. *Note*: MLA stands for Member of Legislative Assembly.

electoral strategies that co-opt the forward or upper-caste groups in order to win elections. The BSP was able to win the 2007 state-level elections in the populous heartland state of Uttar Pradesh by successfully eliciting the support of the upper castes in addition to its traditional support base of scheduled-caste voters.[47]

The political mobilization of the OBCs and the scheduled castes generated a substantial backlash and created a countermobilization strategy on the part of members of higher castes, who believed that this policy would have significant adverse consequences for their employment prospects in the governmental sector. Many violent protests ensued across the country in the wake of the government's announcement that it was going to implement the recommendations of the commission.[48]

Political mobilization also contributed to demands for autonomy and, eventually, secession in Jammu and Kashmir. Substantial political mobilization as a consequence of increased education and media exposure coupled with dramatic institutional decay had left the National Front an unenviable legacy in the disputed Muslim-majority state of Jammu and Kashmir.[49] Ironically enough, significant national investment in health care, education, and mass media had contributed to a new generation of politically conscious Kashmiris. The centralizing and deinstitutionalizing propensities of Indira Gandhi had led to the erosion of political institutions in the state. The convergence of these two factors proved to be a combustible mix. The catalytic event that set off a chain reaction of events culminating in a full-scale insurgency came toward the end of the decade.

---

[47] For a discussion of his strategy, see Chandra, *Why Ethnic Parties Succeed*; also see Sudha Pai, "New Social Engineering Agenda of the Bahujan Samaj Party: Implications for State and National Politics," *South Asia: Journal of South Asian Studies* 2:3 (November 2009): 338–53.

[48] Barbara Crossette, "A Holiday Quiets India after a Week of Rioting," *New York Times*, September 30, 1990.

[49] For a discussion of the origins of political mobilization against a backdrop of institutional decay, see Sumit Ganguly, *The Crisis in Kashmir: Portents of War, Hopes of Peace* (New York: Cambridge University Press, 1997).

The government confronted the beginnings of a major crisis when activists belonging to the separatist Jammu and Kashmir Liberation Front (JKLF) kidnapped Rubiya Sayeed, the daughter of the Union Home Minister Mufti Mohammed Sayeed, in December 1989. The insurgents demanded that the central (national) government release several of their incarcerated members to obtain the safe return of Sayeed's daughter. In a panic, the government conceded the demands of the insurgents in order to obtain her release. Almost immediately after this incident, much of the state of Jammu and Kashmir plunged into a vortex of violence. Though the roots of this ethnoreligious insurgency were indigenous and could be traced to the exigencies of Indian domestic politics, it was quickly transformed as a consequence of Pakistani involvement.[50] During the next several years, various governments in New Delhi were forced to expend considerable blood and treasure as they formulated a viable counterinsurgency strategy in order to suppress the insurgency and restore a modicum of order, if not law, to the state.

The Collapse of the National Front Government

The National Front government fell in 1989 because one of their key parliamentary supporters, the BJP, chose to end its support. The BJP chose to withdraw its parliamentary support largely because it was at odds with the regime regarding the contentious issue of the Babri Masjid, a mosque that had putatively been built on the ruins of a Hindu temple. The temple, BJP activists contend, in turn had consecrated the birthplace of Lord Rama, one of the principal members of the Hindu pantheon.[51]

---

[50] For a discussion of Pakistan's involvement in the insurgency, see Arif Jamal, *Shadow War: The Untold Story of Jihad in Kashmir* (Brooklyn, NY: Melville Press, 2009).

[51] On the Babri Masjid controversy, see S. Gopal, ed., *Anatomy of a Confrontation: The Babri Masjid-Ram Janmabhumi Controversy* (New Delhi: Penguin Books, 1991).

At least two factors had led the BJP to adopt this strategy. At one level, it had chosen to seize on this issue in an attempt to mobilize large numbers of Hindus who were feeling increasingly insecure despite their majority status in the country. Part of this insecurity stemmed from the brutal Punjab insurgency in which Sikh militants had fecklessly and callously targeted Hindus with impunity during much of the 1980s.[52] It also stemmed from a spate of newspaper reports that suggested that the mass conversion of lower-caste Hindus had taken place in the southern Indian state of Tamil Nadu. The BJP leadership carefully stoked these fears and anxieties in an attempt to woo the majority community.[53]

One other factor had led the BJP to embark on this strategy. It was designed as a response to the efforts of the Janata Dal to woo the lower castes to its electoral fold. The V. P. Singh government's decision to resurrect and implement the Mandal Commission Report had drawn significant lower-caste support. Even though lower castes had hardly been a BJP electoral bastion, the prospects of their large-scale identification with another political party was a source of concern.

During the campaign leading up to the next election, the former prime minister, Rajiv Gandhi, was assassinated. The assassin was a woman belonging to the Liberation Tigers of Tamil Eelam (LTTE), a Sri Lankan Tamil extremist group. The LTTE had harbored significant grudges against Rajiv Gandhi because he had not only induced them to accept a peace accord with the Sri Lankan government but also had sent in an Indian peace-keeping force to help monitor the terms of the accord. The mandate of this force, unfortunately,

---

[52] For a discussion of the origins of the Sikh insurgency in the Punjab, see Hamish Telford, "The Political Economy of the Punjab: Creating Space for Sikh Militancy," *Asian Survey* 32:11 (November 1992): 969–87; for its evolution, see Gurharpal Singh, "The Punjab Problem in the 1990s: A Post-1984 Assessment," *Journal of Commonwealth and Comparative Politics* 29:2 (July 1991): 175–91.

[53] For a broader and insightful discussion, see Ashutosh Varshney, "Contested Meanings: India's National Identity, Hindu Nationalism, and the Politics of Anxiety," *Daedalus* 122:3 (Summer 1993): 227–61.

had metamorphosed into peace enforcement when the LTTE had refused to adhere to the stated terms of the accord.[54]

In the wake of Rajiv Gandhi's assassination, the Congress Party again proved to be victorious in the national election. In considerable part, this victory could be attributed to the sympathy that many felt for the Congress Party in the aftermath of his assassination on the campaign trail. A veteran Congress Party politician, Narasimha Rao, assumed office as the new prime minister in 1991. Almost immediately upon assuming office he inherited a major fiscal crisis. His response to the crisis, which was remarkably adept, contributed to a fundamental transformation of India's economic–development strategy, as discussed in Chapter 3.

Much less adroit, however, was his handling of the rising tide of Hindu fanaticism that the BJP had set in motion. Intent on exploiting the sentiments that it had managed to arouse among significant segments of the majority community, the BJP – under the leadership of one of its stalwarts, Lal Krishna Advani – relentlessly pressed the Babri Masjid issue, insisting that the edifice be destroyed and a Hindu temple constructed in its place. To that end, he had undertaken a *rath yatra* since late September 1990.[55] Even though this effort generated considerable support in northern India, leading to the gathering of thousands of supporters in the town of Ayodhya, the Bihar police stopped his assemblage and arrested Advani in the town of Samastipur in late October 1990.

The Irresistible Rise of the Bharatiya Janata Party?

The countermobilization that Advani and the BJP had set in motion in the wake of the Mandal Commission's decision

---

[54] S. D. Muni, *The Pangs of Proximity: India and Sri Lanka's Ethnic Crisis* (New Delhi: Sage Publications, 1993).

[55] The term *rath yatra* connotes a carriage procession in Hindi. Advani's carriage procession from the Somnath temple in Gujarat to the mythical birthplace of Lord Ram in Ayodhya was undertaken in an automobile.

provided a significant electoral boon for the party. In the 1991 national elections, the BJP managed to increase its percentage of the vote to 21 percent from a previous record of 11.4 percent. Most significantly, it now came to command as many as 119 seats in Parliament, which was up from 89.

With this parliamentary majority, the BJP resumed its agitation on the Babri Masjid issue with greater vigor. On December 6, 1992, its most ardent supporters attacked the mosque and destroyed it within a matter of hours. In the aftermath of its destruction, widespread rioting swept across much of northern India and also occurred in the city of Bombay.[56]

Intriguingly enough, the ethnoreligious mobilization strategy seemed to lose steam in the wake of the destruction of the Babri Masjid and the concomitant riots. In November 1993, the BJP lost a series of state elections and was thereby forced to reconsider its electoral strategy. Nevertheless, in the 1996 parliamentary elections it won 20 percent of the popular vote and managed to garner 161 seats in Parliament, emerging as the party with the largest number of seats in the Lok Sabha. As a consequence, it was asked to form the government. However, it proved unable to attract allies and was dissolved within thirteen days. A United Front coalition government composed of fourteen parties replaced the BJP regime, but it lasted a mere eighteen months. In the 1998 elections, the BJP secured 25.5 percent of the popular vote and captured 179 seats in the Lok Sabha. To form a government it still had to woo thirteen political parties. On March 28, 1998, it won a vote of confidence on the floor of Parliament.[57] This was an election in which the Congress Party did not substantially

---

[56] On the Bombay riots, see Asghar Ali Engineer, "Bombay Riots," *PUCL Bulletin*, May 1993, http://www.pucl.org/from-archives/ Religion-communalism/bombay-riots.htm (accessed December 29, 2010); on the riots in northern India, see Pradeep K. Chibber and Subhash Misra, "Hindus and the Babri Masjid: The Sectional Basis of Communal Attitudes," *Asian Survey* 33:7 (July 1993): 665–72.

[57] Robert L. Hardgrave Jr. and Stanley Kochanek, *India: Government and Politics in a Developing Nation* (Boston: Thomson Wadsworth, 2008).

lose its share of seats. Instead, the BJP simply won more seats.
The BJP also demonstrated a superior ability to make alliances
with regional parties like the AIADMK in Tamil Nadu, the
TDP in Andhra Pradesh, the Samata Party in North India,
Lok Shakti in Karnataka, and the Trinamool Congress in West
Bengal. These elections signaled the genesis of a bipolar struc-
ture in Indian politics, in which the Congress Party and the
BJP would constitute the two poles around which coalitions
would be organized.[58]

The second time around, in concert with its parliamentary
allies, the BJP remained in power a full five years. However,
during its stint in office, it either encouraged or at least
tacitly permitted growing attacks on vulnerable minority
populations including the minuscule Christian community in India. At another level, the BJP-led government also
sought to fundamentally alter the terms of political discourse
within the country. To that end, among other matters, it also
embarked on a concerted effort to instill its particular vision
of the Indian polity through efforts involving the drafting
of history and civics texts in Indian schools.[59] The central
goal of the BJP was to inculcate a particular (and parochial)
vision of Indian nationalism through a process of political
socialization in the educational sphere. In turn, it hoped to
create a long-term political base to further its antisecular
political agenda.

Though it helped create permissive conditions for political violence against minorities, the BJP was not able to carry
through the full panoply of its parochial and antisecular electoral platform. For example, it did not seek to abolish Article
370 of the Indian constitution, which grants a special dispensation to Jammu and Kashmir – the only Muslim-majority

---

[58] Sudha Pai, "The Indian Party System under Transformation: Lok Sabha
Elections 1998," *Asian Survey* 38:9 (1998): 836–52.

[59] Marie Lall, "The BJP's Textbook Revisions: What Lasting Legacy
for Society?" *OpinionAsia*, http://opinionasia.com/TheBJPsTextbook
Revisions (accessed December 29, 2010).

state in the Indian Union. Nor, for that matter, did it seek to implement the Uniform Civil Code, which would have abolished Muslim Personal Law.[60] Finally, it did little to resurrect the highly divisive and contentious question of building a temple on the ruins of the Babri Masjid. Most commentators attribute the restraint of the BJP to two factors. First, the party was embedded within a coalition, and several of its members did not share the BJP's antisecular agenda. Second, the exigencies of governing a country as diverse and complex as India also made some of its leadership realize that the single-minded pursuit of such an agenda could come at the cost of pursuing other, more immediate policy concerns.

Nevertheless, a number of deeply disturbing events took place during the BJP's tenure in office. Among other matters, in the state of Gujarat, a pogrom took place against several Muslim communities in February 2002. It is widely believed that BJP chief minister of the state, Narendra Modi, was at least tacitly complicit in allowing the pogrom to proceed.[61] Despite substantial condemnation in the Indian media, Modi's position in Gujarat remained unassailable. He emerged victorious in the 2007 state assembly election, making him the longest-serving chief minister in the state.

In the absence of systematic polling data, it is impossible to assess the precise impact the Gujarat pogrom had on the overall standing of the BJP. However, public commentary suggests that many in India's middle class found the pogrom, along with a growing tide of religious bigotry (which elements of the BJP had encouraged and abetted), to be deeply disturbing, thereby adversely affecting the electoral prospects of the party.

---

[60] For an extensive discussion of the subject of Muslim Personal Law and the Uniform Civil Code, see Partha S. Ghosh, *The Politics of Personal Law in South Asia: Identity, Nationalism and the Uniform Civil Code* (London: Routledge, 2007).

[61] Siddharth Varadarajan, ed., *Gujarat: The Making of a Tragedy* (New Delhi: Penguin Books, 2002).

Political Mobilization and the 2004
and 2009 Elections

The Congress Party–led United Progressive Alliance (UPA) came to power in 2004, thus ending the BJP's seemingly irresistible rise. One of the principal sources of the UPA victory could be traced to its deft strategy of alliances. A variety of other plausible reasons can also be advanced for the BJP's loss in the 2004 elections. These include arguments that the BJP was exclusively a party for rich and upper-caste voters who did not constitute a substantial voting bloc; the Muslim vote may have gone against the BJP in the aftermath of the Gujarat pogrom; and the new social forces, such as backward-caste groups, *dalits*, tribals, and Muslims, may have supported the Congress Party.

Although some of the factors mentioned in the preceding text may have played a role in explaining the BJP's loss in 2004, it seems that the two main reasons for the Congress Party's and the UPA's successes were good luck and a superb coalition strategy. First, although the Congress Party won thirty-one more seats than in the 1999 elections, its vote share actually fell by 1.9 percent. The Congress Party was fortunate in being able to convert its votes into seats more efficiently than the BJP. Second, whereas the Congress Party's allies helped it enormously in terms of vote share and seats, the BJP's allies fared rather poorly. The seats won by the Congress Party's allies went up from twenty-three in 1999 to seventy-six in 2004, and their share in the total votes polled rose from 5.7 percent to 9.4 percent during the same period. The BJP won 138 seats in 2004, which was 44 less than the seats won in 1999. Its allies, who had won 118 seats in 1999, were now able to garner only fifty-one seats. The losses that the TDP of Andhra Pradesh and the AIADMK in Tamil Nadu had registered cost the alliance dearly.[62] The 2009 elections

---

[62] Yogendra Yadav, "The Elusive Mandate of 2004: An Overview," in *Electoral Politics in Indian States*, ed. Sandeep Shastri, K. C. Suri, and

witnessed the further consolidation of the Congress Party and the UPA. This time the Congress Party won 206 seats (61 seats greater than in 2004) in a house of 543 members, making it much less dependent on its allies. The Congress Party's share in the total number of votes polled at 28.56 percent was about 2 percent higher than in 2004, but it remained at about the same level as in 1999 when the Congress Party sat in the opposition.[63] Why then did the Congress Party and the UPA coalition win a comfortable victory in the 2009 elections despite no radical surge in its popularity?

Several plausible reasons seem to account for this convincing victory. First, the Congress Party converted its votes into seats in the Parliament much more efficiently than did the BJP. In 1999, 1 percent of the vote share earned the Congress Party four seats, whereas the same percentage of votes polled for the party in 2009 earned it seven seats in the parliament. Indian parliamentary elections are a series of state-level contests. Analysts point out that votes convert into seats in the Parliament more easily in a particular state when the party crosses a certain threshold of votes in that state. The Congress Party's and the UPA's gains in the 2009 elections was spread over many heavily populated states such as West Bengal, Kerala, Rajasthan, Madhya Pradesh, Punjab, Uttarakhand, and Uttar Pradesh. It was also able to minimize its losses in states such as Tamil Nadu, Andhra Pradesh, Assam, and Haryana.[64]

Second, whereas the Congress Party did only marginally better than in 2009, the BJP fared poorly in this election. The BJP's share of the total votes polled declined from 23.8 percent in 1999 to 18.8 percent in 2009, a figure that was lower than the BJP's vote share in 1991 (20.1%). Even though

Yogendra Yadav (New Delhi: Oxford University Press, 2009), 1–45. This book has detailed chapters explaining the patterns of the 2004 elections in several major Indian states.

[63] Yogendra Yadav and Suhas Palshikar, "Between *Fortuna* and *Virtu*: Explaining the Congress's Ambiguous Victory in 2009," *Economic and Political Weekly* 44:39 (September 26, 2009): 34–6.

[64] Ibid., 36–7.

the Congress Party and the UPA coalition could not create a counterbloc of poor or lower-caste voters against the BJP's vote bank of upper-caste, upper-class, and affluent voters, it was able to draw more votes from the poor and lower-caste groups. Evidence exists to suggest that the UPA's flagship welfare programs (which are discussed at greater length in Chapter 3) led citizens to conclude that the UPA's governance record was superior to that of the National Democratic Alliance (NDA). In addition to this, the NDA lost valuable allies between 2004 and 2009 such as the TDP, the Tamil Manila Congress (Tamil Nadu), the AIADMK, and the Biju Janata Dal (Orissa).[65] And to make matters worse, the BJP and the NDA could not find another charismatic leader of the order of former prime minister Atal Behari Vajpayee. L. K. Advani, the BJP candidate, simply could not match the personal appeal of the Congress Party's candidate – Prime Minister Manmohan Singh.[66]

Do the 2009 parliamentary elections suggest that regional and ethnic mobilization based on caste have become less important for the Indian polity? It seems that that caste-based regionalization of the polity that benefited the NDA during the 1990s has proved to be an advantage for the Congress Party in the new millennium. In Andhra Pradesh, the Praja Rajyam Party ate into the votes of the TDP and contributed to the stellar performance of the Congress Party. The Congress Party and its ally, the Nationalist Congress Party (NCP), gained from the birth of the Maharashtra Navnirman Sena because its creation took votes away from the opposition party Shiv Sena. The Congress Party and the NCP have formed a government together in Maharashtra and the BJP and Shiv Sena have had to sit in the opposition. Other regional allies of the Congress Party such as the Trinamool National Congress (West Bengal) and the DMK also fared

---

[65] Ibid., 33–7, 42–4. On the governance record of the Congress Party, see K. C. Suri, "The Economy and Voting in the 15th Lok Sabha Elections," *Economic and Political Weekly* 44:39 (September 26, 2009): 64–70.

[66] Yadav and Palshikar, "Between *Fortuna* and *Virtu*," 44.

well. Although the BSP, the *dalit* party in opposition (based largely in the populous state of Uttar Pradesh), fared poorly compared to popular expectations, it still polled the highest number of votes in the state (27.4%).[67] Even when in decline, the BJP was able to maintain its lead over the Congress Party in upper-caste Hindu votes. However, in the 2004 and 2009 elections, the Congress Party's electoral gains within this group were greater than its gains in other groups.[68]

Conclusions

The political mobilization that is currently under way in the country, and especially in northern India, promises to alter the physiognomy of India's democracy in the years and decades ahead. As a number of scholars have shown, a social revolution swept through many of India's southern states during the 1960s. This involved the rise of lower castes and the demise of a Brahmin-dominated sociopolitical order.[69] A markedly similar process of political mobilization is now under way in northern India albeit under somewhat different circumstances.[70]

Three disturbing features of the current wave of political mobilization exist. First, it is taking place against a backdrop of political institutions that, to a very significant extent, have been corroded. A similar wave of political mobilization had taken place in southern India during the 1960s. However, at that time, the country had far more robust and durable political

---

[67] Jaffrelot and Verniers, "India's 2009 Elections," 1–20. See *South Asia Multidisciplinary Academic Journal*, http://samaj.revues.org/index2787. html (accessed December 29, 2010).

[68] Yadav and Palshikar, "Between *Fortuna* and *Virtu*," 41.

[69] For the classic study, see Robert L. Hardgrave Jr., *The Nadars of Tamilnad* (Berkeley: University of California Press, 1969); also see James Manor, "Karnataka," in Frankel and Rao, *Dominance and State Power in Modern India*.

[70] See the discussion in Ashutosh Varshney, "Is India Becoming More Democratic?" *Journal of Asian Studies* 59:1 (February 2000): 3–24.

institutions and their capacity to absorb the rising cacophony of demands was considerable. Under the present institutional dispensation, however, the institutions simply do not possess the resilience to cope with these demands. Worse still, key political leaders, most notably Kumari Mayawati, the chief minister of Uttar Pradesh, have done much to undermine further the probity and viability of existing political institutions and their norms through high-handed and nepotistic behavior when dealing with bureaucrats and administrators, the pursuit of a variety of populist schemes, and fiscal irresponsibility.[71] The debility of institutions and rising levels of political consciousness and demands for participation can result in political instability, which would further strain institutional resources and capacity.

Perhaps the most egregious example of this form of political mobilization took place under the long reign (1990–7) of a politically adroit, populist, and allegedly corrupt politician, Laloo Prasad Yadav, in the state of Bihar. During his tenure, he pursued recklessly populist politics, urged lower castes to stand up to high-caste oppression, and used state power fecklessly in an effort to advance his putative social agenda of empowering the dispossessed and the socially marginalized. However, these efforts were largely woven around his flamboyant personality, and he evinced scant regard for institutional procedures and norms. Furthermore, though the charges were never successfully prosecuted, a series of allegations involving dubious spending from the state exchequer were leveled against him.[72] His style of governance contributed to the decay of political institutions throughout the state even while it contributed to the political mobilization of lower castes and minorities.[73]

---

[71] Jackie Range, "Mayawati Mystique Rejected by Voters," *Wall Street Journal*, May 18, 2009.

[72] Times News Network, "Laloo to Face Separate Trials in Fodder Scam," *The Times of India*, August 27, 2003.

[73] For an excellent account of the underlying structural problems of the state that were exacerbated through populist policies, see Kohli, *Democracy and Discontent*.

Second, from a normative standpoint, the political mobilization of hitherto socially marginalized segments of the population and their increased participation may be desirable for a democratic state.[74] However, from the perspective of civic governance, this form of political mobilization along ethnic lines can also have highly undesirable consequences for a democratic and civic polity. There is little question that India's poor and dispossessed need to be woken from what Marx called the "sleep of ages." The emphasis on group and caste mobilization will inevitably produce new waves of social tensions and conflict.

In a related vein, this wave of political mobilization that raises questions about India's democratic future is its emphasis on group rights as opposed to individual rights. The demands being expressed are cast entirely in the form of group entitlements. Such an emphasis on group rights, although understandable from the standpoint of India's lower castes, nevertheless may have two potentially adverse consequences. An emphasis on group rights overlooks important class divisions within lower castes, and thereby fails to address questions of their material advancement.[75]

Third, an emphasis on group identities will, in all likelihood, also have the unintended consequence of reifying caste. Resultantly, far from producing a society in which age-old caste distinctions are steadily effaced and increasingly seen as atavistic forms of social organization, the politics of group mobilization will ensure that this primordial vision will continue to thrive, albeit under different social and political circumstances. This is a question that social activists and scholars alike must ponder.

[74] The earliest and most cogent statement of this conundrum remains that of Samuel Huntington, *Political Order in Changing Societies* (New Haven, CT: Yale University Press, 1968).

[75] For a trenchant discussion of these issues, see Zoya Hasan, "Representation and Redistribution: The New Lower Caste Politics of North India," in *Transforming India: Social and Political Dynamics of Democracy*, ed. Francine R. Frankel, Zoya Hasan, Rajeev Bhargava, and Balveer Arora (New Delhi: Oxford University Press, 2000).

The forces of social mobilization that have been unleashed in India as a consequence of the country's routine elections at local, state, and national levels, coupled with growing levels of literacy and media exposure, are likely to alter the very physiognomy of the Indian state in the years and decades ahead. The dominance of a caste-based social order is being fundamentally upended even if it is generating a substantial political backlash.[76] Nevertheless, the promise of Indian democracy, despite multiple setbacks and periodic backsliding, is being steadily realized. One useful indicator is the changing social background of legislators in the Indian Parliament. For example, it is instructive to compare data from the tenth and fourteenth Lok Sabhas. In the tenth Lok Sabha (1991), there were ninety-nine individuals from the backward castes. The figure rose to 118 in the fourteenth Lok Sabha (2004), constituting a growth of 3 percent. Simultaneously, upper-caste representation showed a decline of 2 percent. Admittedly, these changes can hardly be described as dramatic. Nevertheless, they are reflective of deeper social changes that are under way in the Indian polity.

---

[76] For a discussion of the upending of the caste-based social order, see Myron Weiner, "The Struggle for Equality: Caste in Indian Politics," in *The Success of India's Democracy*, ed. Atul Kohli (Cambridge: Cambridge University Press, 2001).

5

Indian Secularism Since 1980

As India enters the twenty-first century, one of the key pillars of its constitutional democracy – the commitment to secularism – remains shaky. It remains infirm despite the defeat of the Hindu nationalist Bharatiya Janata Party (BJP)–led coalition in two successive national elections (2004 and 2009).[1] The ideologues within the BJP and its associated organizations, most notably the Rashtriya Swayamsevak Sangh (RSS) and the Vishwa Hindu Parishad (VHP), have not abandoned their staunchly antisecular orientation. On the contrary, they have argued with some vigor that the failure of the BJP to prevail in both of the elections stems from its unwillingness to firmly uphold the values of "Hindutva." They contend that a robust assertion of the core principles of the party would have held it in good electoral stead.[2] The appointment of a new president, Nitin Gadkari, who has his roots in the RSS, suggests that the party is hardly about to disavow its antisecular credo.[3] Given the perfervid commitment of party ideologues to this antisecular vision, it would be premature to

---

[1] Jo Johnson, "A Creed of Loathe Thy Neighbor," *Financial Times*, March 31/April 1, 2007.

[2] B. S. Satish Kumar, "No Compromise on Hindutva Despite Poll Debacle: Rajnath," *The Hindu*, August 2, 2009.

[3] Vinay Kumar, "Nitin Gadkari Is BJP Chief," *The Hindu*, December 20, 2009.

assume that the danger that the BJP and its political allies pose to Indian secularism is at an end.[4]

A postelection controversy involving a stalwart member of the BJP, Jaswant Singh, a former minister of finance and minister of external affairs (foreign minister), underscored the party's unwillingness to countenance any significant dissent regarding the critical question of its core ideological beliefs. A brief discussion of this controversy illuminates the intransigence of the party toward the question of secularism. Singh, a noted parliamentarian and a long-term member of the BJP, was not known for his virulent antisecular orientation. On the contrary, he had a scholarly mien, and his principal interests had been in the realms of foreign and security policy, which reflected his prior military background. Singh had previously written several books on Indian politics and foreign policy.

His publication of a book on the life of the founder of Pakistan, Mohammed Ali Jinnah, *Jinnah-Partition-Independence*, led to his ouster from the BJP in mid-August of 2009. The book's criticism of some key figures of the Indian independence movement, notably Sardar Vallabhbhai Patel, was the principal reason for his ouster from the party.[5] Shortly thereafter, the western Indian state of Gujarat also banned the book on the same grounds. Quite apart from his historical standing, Patel is still seen an important political icon in his home state.

Jaswant Singh's enforced departure from the BJP no doubt represents the triumph of the more unyielding ideologues within the party. The question that remains is whether these ideologues will continue to hold sway over the workings of the party as it plots its way toward the next national election. Singh, though committed to a muscular foreign and

---

[4] For an especially thoughtful and detailed account of the BJP's antisecular stance, see Paranjoy Guha Thakurta and Shankar Raghuraman, *Divided We Stand: India in a Time of Coalitions* (New Delhi: Sage Publications, 2007), 156–239.

[5] Editorial, "Making Sense of Jinnah Today," *Economic and Political Weekly* 44:34 (August 22, 2009): 5.

security policy and an ardent Indian nationalist, was obviously not wedded to the party's viciously antisecular agenda. His departure and the dominance of those who remain true to the party's central creed will, in considerable measure, determine the future political prospects of the party. Whether its relentless antisecular agenda, coupled with a virulently nationalist appeal, will enable it to make much headway in India's national politics is difficult to predict. However, unless it sheds its antisecular ethos, it will remain a genuine threat to the well-being of India's liberal-democratic prospects.

Before turning to a discussion of the challenges that the BJP and others posed to the workings of Indian secularism since 1980, it is necessary to provide a brief historical background to the origins, development, and evolution of Indian secularism.[6] Contrary to what many may think, neither Indian secularism nor Indian democracy is something that the Indians passively received from British colonialism. The British did little during their two centuries of rule over the subcontinent to promote either democracy or secularism. Both are best understood less as British bequests than as Indian appropriations. Indian nationalist leaders, and above all the Harrow-trained Jawaharlal Nehru, consciously decided to borrow certain liberal and pluralist tenets from European thought and historical experience and plant them as principles meant to guide Indian political life.[7] It was an admirable,

---

[6] For a somewhat idiosyncratic historical account of the origins of Indian secularism, see Shabnum Tejani, *Indian Secularism: A Social and Intellectual History, 1890–1950* (New Delhi: Permanent Black, 2007); the classic statement on the origins of Indian secularism remains Donald Eugene Smith, *India as a Secular State* (Princeton, NJ: Princeton University Press, 1963); for a critique of the practice of Indian secularism, see Prakash Chandra Upadhyaya, "The Politics of Indian Secularism," *Modern Asian Studies* 26:4 (October 1992): 815–53.

[7] For an excellent analysis of the rise of secularism in Europe, see Owen Chadwick, *The Secularization of the European Mind in the Nineteenth Century* (Cambridge: Cambridge University Press, 1975). For a discussion of Nehru's signal contributions, see Sarvepalli Gopal, *Jawaharlal Nehru: A Biography* (Cambridge, MA: Harvard University Press, 1976).

courageous, and highly intelligent act of creative adoption –
undeterred by the shameful yet ultimately immaterial fact
that Europeans often honored such tenets more in the breach
than the observance when running their colonies – and India
as well as the world have been much better off for it.

During the era of activism on behalf of independence,
the principle of secularism hardly ruled the Indian political
arena uncontested. The principal nationalist group, the Indian
National Congress, from the 1930s on managed to build a
mass anticolonial movement but never quite succeeded in
bringing every group under its umbrella or bridging all the
major divisions in Indian society. The reasons for failure were
complicated. The apparently primordial Hindu institution of
caste had riddled Indian society with wide and deep cleavages,
as had the checkered history of Hindu-Muslim relations.

Certain colonial practices, some adopted out of an aim to
divide and rule and others for reasons of administrative convenience, exacerbated the splits among Indians. The British-
run census, for instance, used classifications that reinforced
caste distinctions among the Hindu majority. Similarly, British
willingness to create communal electorates during the early
part of the twentieth century reinforced Hindu-Muslim
political differences. As independence approached in 1947,
the demands of electoral politics led Congress to compromise its secularist principles. Finally, by introducing European
mores, customs, and values, British colonial rule inadvertently
stimulated various Hindu revivalist movements that sprang up
in reaction.[8]

As the constitution of newly independent India was being
drafted (ratification came in 1950), disagreements over secularism welled up. Although most of the framers were secularists, some members of the Constituent Assembly did harbor
strong majoritarian religious sentiments and opposed the idea
of a religiously neutral state. More generally, the framers had to

---

[8] For one useful discussion, see Christophe Jaffrelot, *The Hindu Nationalist Movement in India* (New Delhi: Penguin Books, 1996).

confront the challenge of fashioning a secular constitution in order to govern a society deeply suffused with a variety of religious sentiments.[9] Difficulties notwithstanding, the end result was a constitution that recognized the rights of religious minorities, did not privilege the majority Hindu system of custom and belief, and granted freedom of religion to all citizens "subject to public order, morality and health."[10]

It should also be noted that the constitution the framers produced was not religiously neutral. On the contrary, it contained explicit provisions abolishing certain retrograde features of Hindu society, namely, those associated with the practice of "untouchability." Indian secularism, as one scholar puts it, is ameliorative.[11] Ironically, this ameliorative impulse has helped to reinforce caste distinctions. Hoping to redress past injustices, India's postindependence leaders started various affirmative-action or "positive discrimination" programs, most notably in regard to college admissions and government jobs. Not surprisingly, numerous politicians now make blatant caste-based appeals.

At another level, subsequently a number of framers, who were also members of the ruling Congress Party, introduced legislation that transformed Hindu personal law in the realms of marriage, divorce, and inheritance. Yet the same legislators made a conscious effort to avoid changing Muslim personal law, concluding that the still-fresh trauma of partition made it advisable to defer legal reform of the Muslim minority's religious practices to a later time. This decision to defer the reform of Muslim personal law would later play into the hands of Hindu zealots and political activists who could disingenuously argue that the officially secular state was actually

---

[9] James Chiriyankandath, "Creating a Secular State in a Religious Country: The Debate in the Indian Constituent Assembly," *Journal of Commonwealth and Comparative Politics* 38:2 (July 2000): 1–24.

[10] See the discussion in Thomas Pantham, "Indian Secularism and Its Critics: Some Reflections," *The Review of Politics* 59:3 (Summer 1997): 523–40.

[11] Gary Jeffrey Jacobsohn, *The Wheel of Law: India's Secularism in Comparative Constitutional Context* (Princeton, NJ: Princeton University Press, 2003).

a scheme for pandering to minorities.[12] The question continues to roil Indian politics. In July 2003, the Supreme Court nonbindingly endorsed the idea of a uniform civil law for all religious communities. Every major camp reacted predictably: the BJP praised the court, the opposition Congress Party suggested that such legislation should not be imposed on minority religious communities, and Muslim spokesmen suggested that only Islamic scholars could be competent in such an area.[13]

Is India, home to nearly a sixth of humanity, still a place where citizens can count on being treated equally, regardless of their religious or communal identity? On February 27, 2002, a group of Hindu activists boarded a train leaving the city of Ayodhya in the populous north Indian state of Uttar Pradesh. They had gone there for a ceremony to mark the start of work on a temple at a disputed religious site. Back in December 1992, Hindu militants with ties to the BJP and its affiliates had descended on Ayodhya for the purpose of razing the Babri Masjid, a centuries-old mosque that, so they claimed, the Muslim rulers of an earlier day had erected after tearing down a major Hindu temple on the spot.

While the train lay at a stop in the town of Godhra, in the state of Gujarat along India's northwestern coast, local Muslims set fire to the railcars, burning fifty-eight people to death. Within days of this atrocity, well-organized Hindu mobs were systematically attacking Muslims and Muslim-owned businesses in various parts of Gujarat. The BJP-run state government of Chief Minister Narendra Modi took days to act, by which time several thousand Muslims had lost their lives. Some Hindu militants sought to justify this pogrom by pointing to the Muslim train attack.[14] Later, credible

---

[12] Ibid., 286.

[13] Reuters, "Indian Court Urges Common Personal Laws," July 24, 2003.

[14] Celia W. Dugger, "Hindu Justifies Mass Killings of Muslims in Reprisal Riots," *New York Times*, March 5, 2002, A4. For more on the Gujarat pogrom of early 2002, see the Ethics and Public Policy Center's *Center Conversations* transcript, "Hindu Nationalism vs. Islamic Jihad: Religious

allegations would surface that officials in Modi's government were complicit in acts of arson and mayhem.

According to India's constitution, national officials can dismiss a state government if they determine that state officials are failing to maintain law and order. The orchestrated attacks on Muslims in many parts of Gujarat and the near-complete – and to all appearances willful – failure of the state government to put a quick stop to the carnage should have been grounds for dismissal. In the event, the BJP-led coalition government of Prime Minister A. B. Vajpayee in New Delhi refused to suspend or even criticize Modi. Instead, the government embraced him and permitted him to campaign for fresh elections in his home state and beyond. The BJP handily won Gujarat state elections in December 2002. Though Modi's appeal outside his home state was limited, he also played a role in the BJP's election strategy in the state of Himachal Pradesh that year. What is especially disturbing is Modi's continuing popularity within the BJP and within his home state. He has largely achieved this iconic status through a thoroughly technocratic and autocratic mode of governance. According to a particularly thoughtful analysis, much of his popularity can be ascribed to his ability to improve material conditions within his state through his deft courtship of investment and improvements in the state's physical infrastructure.[15]

The crimes of commission and omission in Gujarat notwithstanding, the constitutional dispensation of Indian secularism remains intact, and its practice is not dead – yet. But its health is poor, and it may be facing a slow demise. The stakes are huge. If secularism breaks down decisively in India, this will spell the rise of "illiberal democracy" in that country

Militancy in South Asia: A Conversation with Cedric Prakash, Teesta Setalvad, Kamal Chenoy, Sumit Ganguly, Sunil Khilnani, and Jonah Blank," www.eppc.org/publications/pubID.1533/pub_detail.asp (accessed December 27, 2010); also see Siddharth Varadarajan, ed., *Gujarat: The Making of a Tragedy* (New Delhi: Penguin Books, 2002).

[15] Ashok V. Desai, "The Education of Modi: An Unreflective Autocrat," *The Telegraph*, March 10, 2009.

and raise grave questions about the sustainability of liberal democracy across the entire postcolonial world.[16] In the most immediate practical terms, the rise of a purely majoritarian democracy amid India's cultural, religious, and ethnic heterogeneity would consign hundreds of millions of people to a dubious political future with little or no security for even their most basic rights. In the worst case, it could mean bloody strife on an unprecedented scale between militants from India's 82 percent Hindu majority and their opposite numbers from minorities such as the Muslims, who make up about 12 percent of India's population of more than one billion people. Therefore, it is important to pay close attention to the sources and the likely trajectory of illiberal sectarian politics in India.

The Secular Record

For the first several decades after independence and partition, the Indian National Congress thoroughly dominated politics, and the party's wide aegis covered a varied array of opinions and interests.[17] Not all members of Congress were committed to secular principles. Many, including Nehru's successor as prime minister, Lal Bahadur Shastri (1964–6), were inclined to favor Hindu primacy. Nevertheless, the constitutional commitment to secularism, large numbers of votes to be found among Muslims, and presence of numerous dedicated secularists in party ranks kept the Congress loyal to secular principles and practices.

---

[16] For a discussion of this concept, see Fareed Zakaria, *The Future of Freedom: Illiberal Democracy at Home and Abroad* (New York: W. W. Norton, 2003); Robert Kagan, "Idealism without Apologies: Why There's No Such Thing as Too Much Democracy," *New Republic*, July 7 and 14, 2003, 27–37.

[17] The Indian political scientist Rajni Kothari dubbed this the "Congress system." See Rajni Kothari, *Politics in India* (Boston: Little, Brown, 1970).

Moreover, the principal antisecular party, the Bharatiya Jana Sangh (BJS, the predecessor to the BJP), failed to attract many adherents and hence posed only a minor electoral challenge. The BJS's shortcomings as a vote-getter came in part from its dubious ties to the Hindu radicalism of the RSS, an organization that had been implicated in the January 1948 assassination of Mohandas K. Gandhi. The BJS also held little attraction for India's lower-caste Hindus or minorities because of its upper-caste Hindu orientation and explicitly antiminority rhetoric.

The Congress Party's political dominance began to slip during the late 1960s, and with it India's secular principles began to be sapped. In 1967, the post-Nehru Congress Party suffered a significant defeat at the polls on issues of personality and substance, and it soon split in two. Nehru's daughter, Indira Gandhi, had become prime minister upon Shastri's sudden death of natural causes in early 1966, and she played a significant role in engineering this schism. By the early 1970s, Gandhi had tenuously restored the Congress Party to a leading position by making populist promises to abolish poverty. But her triumph was fleeting. Under her tutelage, the Congress Party and most of India's political institutions fell into disarray. Whereas her father had played a signal role in building up key institutions from the independent judiciary to the robust party system, Indira Gandhi engineered their decline.[18]

The full reasons for her attack on India's institutions are highly complex. In a nutshell, her populist rhetoric and practices stirred a wave of mass political mobilization. From her vantage atop its crest, she saw established institutions – including the independent judiciary and civil service as well as the democratic internal procedures of her party – as

[18] Even one of the staunchest critics of Indian democracy concedes that Nehru's role in promoting India's institutional development was exemplary. See Zakaria, *The Future of Freedom*; also see Susanne Hoeber Rudolph and Lloyd Rudolph, "Congress Learns to Lose: From a One-Party Dominant to a Multiparty System in India." Paper presented at the annual meeting of the American Political Science Association, Washington, DC, September 1, 2005.

barriers to her goal of prevailing politically at the head of a securely dominant Congress Party. Hence she launched an assault on these institutions and engaged in reckless abuse of such constitutional prerogatives as the right to dismiss state governments.[19]

Secularism, a cornerstone of the Indian constitutional order and a principle that the Congress Party under Nehru had mostly championed, was another set of restraints to be opportunistically knocked aside by Indira Gandhi's electoral surge. There was a double irony here, for not only had her father been among secularism's founders, but also her own personal commitment to secularism was never in doubt.[20] Her actions against the secular enterprise cannot be separated from her general hostility toward constitutional proprieties or her willingness to thwart the rule of law when votes were at stake.

Gandhi's willingness to overstep the bounds of constitutional propriety on secularism and other matters created space for the rapid rise of an antisecular alternative. The BJS was the leading candidate for the role. Founded formally in 1951, but with roots that stretched back to the 1920s and the early years of such militant Hindu organizations as the RSS and Mahasabha, BJS had its social base among the upper-caste Hindus of north India.[21] The group had long viewed itself as the Congress Party's rival for the allegiance of India's Hindu majority and had always taken an anti-Muslim, anti-Pakistan

---

[19] Paul R. Brass, *The Politics of India since Independence* (Cambridge: Cambridge University Press, 1994).

[20] E.g., even after the rise of violent Sikh separatism in the Punjab and the Indian Army's attack on the Golden Temple in Amritsar, the holiest Sikh shrine, she refused to dispense with her Sikh bodyguards. She explicitly stated that in a secular state the removal of her bodyguards on the basis of their faith would convey an infelicitous political symbolism. See Stephanie Nolen, "Invoking Indira," *The Toronto Globe and Mail*, October 31, 2009.

[21] For a historical analysis of the rise of the Jana Sangh and its affiliated organizations, see Bruce Desmond Graham, *Hindu Nationalism and Indian Politics: The Origins and Development of the Bharatiya Jana Sangh* (Cambridge: Cambridge University Press, 1990).

stance. Despite a strong economic-nationalist strain in the BJS's ranks, it was more sympathetically inclined toward market-oriented economic policies than was the Congress Party, which leaned socialist.

During 1975 and 1976, Indira Gandhi declared "emergency" rule, allowing her to seize power in a kind of executive self-coup and trample civil liberties in the process. The 1977 election turned her out of power and left the Congress Party in disarray. As part of these events, the BJS had merged briefly with other groups in order to create the short-lived Janata (People's) Party and to rule as part of a governing coalition that hung on shakily until 1980. When voters swept Indira Gandhi back into power that year, the new BJP, with the old BJS cadres at its core, emerged out of the Janata coalition's wreckage.[22] Ever since then, the BJP has been the antisecularist standard-bearer. Around it swirls an alphabet soup of mass-based groups, including not only the RSS but also the VHP and the Bajrang Dal (the VHP's youth wing, founded in 1984). Together, the whole collection – BJP plus affiliates – is known as the Sangh Parivar.

Three Episodes and Their Import

A series of events, some accidental, others deliberate, tore at Indian secularism beginning in the 1980s and allowed the emergence of antisecular politics. Three episodes in particular stand out as deliberate choices that undermined the secular order: Indira Gandhi's political courtship of a violent Sikh fundamentalist preacher in the early 1980s; the 1986 decision of her son and political heir, Rajiv Gandhi, to overturn a critical decision of the Supreme Court on Muslim personal

---

[22] Robert L. Hardgrave Jr., "Hindu Nationalism and the BJP: Transforming Religion and Politics in India," in *Prospects of Peace in South Asia*, ed. Rafiq Dossani and Henry S. Rowen (Stanford: Stanford University Press, 2005), 193.

law; and the failure of the Congress Party government of Prime Minister Narasimha Rao to stop a Hindu nationalist mob from tearing down Ayodhya's Babri Masjid in 1992.[23]

The unraveling of the secularist fabric started with the rise of demands for regional autonomy in the Punjab – a northwestern border state, divided with Pakistan during partition, that had a slender Sikh majority – and the manner in which the Indian state under Indira Gandhi responded to those demands. A desire for regional autonomy had long made itself felt in the Punjab, but the constitutional order and the practice of Indian federalism had managed to contain this desire during the first three decades of independence. Then came the 1980s, with their confluence of greater mass political mobilization and an increasingly ossified Congress Party; factors that together fueled the rise of regional parties across the vast breadth of the subcontinent. The local manifestation of this phenomenon in the Punjab struck Indira Gandhi with special force. She detected in the appearance and rhetoric of the regional Akali Dal party not only a threat to the Congress Party's dominance but also a strong whiff of secessionism. In a perverse attempt to undermine the growing popularity of the Akalis, she chose actively to court and encourage a violent, fundamentalist Sikh preacher, Jarnail Singh Bhindranwale, who had political ambitions of his own and proved to be more than a match for her. Soon he and his followers had turned their wrath against the Hindus of the Punjab, terrorizing them at will and killing hundreds, often by sending motorcycle-riding terrorists to spray crowds with deadly machine-gun fire.

Not surprisingly, these rampant attacks on Hindus, orchestrated by Bhindranwale from the Golden Temple in Amritsar, the holiest of Sikh shrines, led to a Hindu backlash across northern India and helped solidify an otherwise atomistic set of communities. Worse still, the communal violence created a whole new rift in Indian society – between Hindus and Sikhs.

[23] Hardgrave, "Hindu Nationalism and the BJP."

Unable to contain Bhindranwale's terror campaign, Gandhi ordered the army to attack the temple in June 1984. The military operation on the night of June 5 proved costly in human and political terms. As many as a thousand people were killed, among them Bhindranwale, and the attack inflamed even moderate Sikhs, who construed it as an assault on their faith.

On October 31, the prime minister's own Sikh bodyguards assassinated her. In response, Hindu mobs with links to the Congress Party went on a systematic rampage, slaughtering Sikhs at will throughout the capital city of New Delhi. This pogrom, which cost thousands of lives, did not stop until the army was called out to restore order several days into November.[24] Indira Gandhi's willingness to court religious zealots in order to achieve dubious short-term political ends had contributed not only to her own demise but also to the deaths of several hundred Hindus and many more Sikhs. The complicity of the Congress Party in the revenge killing of Sikhs showed the danger and doubt that now shadowed the practice of secularism.

The assault on secularism and the disregard that Indira Gandhi had evinced for institutions would continue under her inexperienced son and successor, Rajiv Gandhi, albeit in a more complex and convoluted fashion. Some of the same imperatives drove mother and son. Like her, he was a secularist personally, but found the idea of scoring quick electoral gains by tampering with secularist institutions and norms too tempting a prospect to turn down.

The Problem of Muslim Personal Law

The second major step in the unraveling of the secular order was the Shah Bano case, which began in 1985. Shah Bano

[24] On the role of the police during the 1984 riots, see Vrinda Grover, "Role of Police in Anti-Sikh Massacre, Delhi," in *Minorities and Police in India*, ed. Asghar Ali Engineer and Amarjit S. Narang (New Delhi: Manohar, 2006).

was an indigent and divorced Muslim woman who appealed to the Indian Supreme Court under Section 125 of the Code of Criminal Procedure. She wanted the court to overrule her ex-husband's claim that Muslim personal law exempted him from having to pay her alimony. The court ruled that, despite the existence of a separate Muslim personal law, the husband was obliged under Indian criminal law to make the alimony payments.[25] The court's opinion was in line with the ameliorative tradition in Indian secularism. According to this view, state authorities could actively intervene, in the name of supreme public values such as equal justice, to change deeply embedded and historically sanctioned practices, even when some people claimed religious sanction for such practices. Thus the laws of modern India had altered Hindu inheritance customs and done away with untouchability.[26]

In reality, things could not be this simple. The court's judgment in the Shah Bano case angered many Indian Muslims. Leading Muslim politicians insisted vociferously that their personal law was now in danger. A dramatic surge in political mobilization among Muslims nationwide occurred, especially in north India. Also fueling this mobilization were growing ties between certain Indian Muslims and their coreligionists in the Persian Gulf states.[27] During the oil-boom years of the 1970s and 1980s, many (often skilled) Indian Muslims took high-paying jobs in the Gulf region and came home flush with previously unheard-of wealth and a much-greater readiness to assert the claims of their community. To accommodate the Muslim ferment, Rajiv Gandhi used his parliamentary

[25] For an especially nuanced discussion of the nexus of religion and politics, see Kavita R. Khory, "The Shah Bano Case: Some Political Implications," in *Religion and Law in Independent India*, ed. Robert D. Baird (New Delhi: Manohar, 1993), 149–67.

[26] For a particularly detailed and comparative discussion, see Partha S. Ghosh, *The Politics of Personal Law in South Asia: Identity, Nationalism and the Uniform Civil Code* (London: Routledge, 2007).

[27] Thomas Blom Hansen, *The Saffron Wave: Democracy and Hindu Nationalism in Modern India* (Princeton, NJ: Princeton University Press, 1999).

majority to grant Muslims a separate dispensation in matters of marriage and divorce.

The decision to overturn the court's ruling had unsettling consequences, however. It made significant sections of the Hindu majority feel more vulnerable – especially in north India, home to most of India's more than one hundred million Muslims and the focus of the Sikh-separatist terror campaign. The BJP courted these jittery Hindu voters skillfully, playing on their resentment at seeing the Congress Party so ready to pander to minority sentiments. As L. K. Advani later commented, the bill "was a watershed event....The mood of the Hindus began building up after [it]."[28] Grasping the danger of a backlash from Hindu voters, advisers to Rajiv Gandhi concluded that they needed to assuage the majority's anxieties. Sadly, the method that they chose would badly wound Indian secularism yet again.

The issue that the Congress Party decided to highlight touched on the most primeval elements of Indian culture and society.[29] Most practicing Hindus believe that Ayodhya in Uttar Pradesh, India's most populous state, is the birthplace of Lord Rama, the legendary hero-king who, together with his three half-brothers, is believed to have made up the seventh avatar or incarnation of the Hindu god Vishnu. Ever since the nineteenth century, Hindu activists had been claiming that a sixteenth-century mosque (the Babri Masjid) built there by the Mogul emperor Babur stood on the spot of an earlier Hindu temple – allegedly torn down by Muslims – marking Lord Rama's exact birthplace. Hindus had sought to build a new temple in the vicinity during the British Raj, but colonial authorities stopped them. Not long after independence, in December 1949, Hindu zealots placed icons of Lord Rama within the Babri Masjid's sanctuary. Fearing religious discord, the Nehru government in Delhi sent word

---

[28] Advani as quoted in Upadhyaya, "The Politics of Indian Secularism," 844.
[29] For scholarly analyses of this controversy see Sarvepalli Gopal, ed., *Anatomy of a Confrontation* (New Delhi: Viking, 1991).

to state and local officials that the icons would have to go. The local magistrate refused and was eventually sacked. The Uttar Pradesh state government left the icons in place but sealed the mosque to head off trouble. Thereafter the issue lay mostly dormant, despite occasional Muslim lawsuits and Hindu agitations.[30]

The decision by Rajiv Gandhi's government to make a national issue of this dispute between two religions over a single piece of holy ground was entirely deliberate and calculating. The Ayodhya conflict did not just happen – it was engineered. The opportunity began to take shape in 1985, when the Hindu militants of the VHP reacted to the Muslim mobilization that followed the Shah Bano case by launching a mass agitation to demand the unsealing of the Babri Masjid. During early 1986, a local lawyer with no previous role in any of the old cases began petitioning the courts for this purpose. A local judge agreed with him on appeal and ordered the mosque unlocked. Serious observers familiar with these events insist that the judge acted at the behest of certain local Congress Party stalwarts – again underscoring the decline of institutional and judicial probity at local levels.

The BJP and its affiliates started a nationwide campaign to demolish the mosque and construct a Hindu temple in its place, urging people from across India to send bricks to Ayodhya for this end. Not to be outdone, the Congress Party resorted to symbolic gestures aimed at arousing Hindu feelings. Among other things, it arranged for the state-run television network to serialize a version of the *Ramayana* (or story of Rama), one of the two great Hindu epics; launched a local electoral campaign from Faizabad, a town near Ayodhya; and allowed the foundation stones of the proposed temple to be laid near the mosque.[31]

---

[30] For an excellent collection of documents on the origins and evolution of the Babri Masjid controversy, see A. G. Noorani, *The Babri Masjid Question: 1528–2003*, vols. 1 and 2 (New Delhi: Tulika Books, 2003)

[31] Partha S. Ghosh, *The Rise of Political Hinduism in India* (Ebenhausen, Germany: Stiftung Wissenschaft und Politik, 1995).

The Ayodhya Crisis Mounts

The events of the late 1980s were tumultuous as the BJP and its allies stepped up the pressure to build a temple in Ayodhya, receiving in the process a good deal of support from northern India's Hindu voters. From the 1984 to the 1989 national elections, the BJP went from just two to eighty-eight parliamentary seats. Rajiv Gandhi and the Congress Party, meanwhile, failed even to gesture toward pursuing a countermobilization strategy based on the reaffirmation of secular principles such as freedom and tolerance, giving the BJP all the moral and political space it needed to push its viciously antisecular agenda.

Contingent events also helped the BJP. The 1989 elections saw the Congress Party routed, but no single successor party emerged. The BJP wound up forming a loose and unlikely alliance with V. P. Singh's left-of-center National Front, offering parliamentary support without actually joining the cabinet. The strains within this marriage of convenience began to show as soon as the National Front, eager to secure its lower-caste base, put in motion a sweeping affirmative-action plan that called for 27 percent of all government jobs and higher educational places to be set aside for applicants belonging to what in Indian bureaucratese are known as members of the Other Backward Classes (OBC). The reaction against this so-called Mandal Plan (after the chairperson of the commission that suggested it) proved to be swift and violent, resulting even in the self-immolation of some university students.

The stir placed the BJP in a tricky position between its middle- and upper-caste base (which was furious over the Mandal Commission Report) and the lower-caste voters whom the party was trying to woo. In the end, loyalty to the base won out. In September 1990, BJP stalwart Lal Krishna Advani embarked on a national trek (*rath yatra*) in a Toyota truck bedecked to look like a chariot from the ancient Hindu epic the *Mahabharata*. Trailing clouds of nostalgia for Hindu martial glory, Advani's caravan caused waves of excitement among BJP backers across northern India. This was, without question, a BJP strategy of countermobilization designed to undermine the caste-based appeal of the Mandal Commission Report. After outbreaks of ethnoreligious violence, a worried Singh government had Advani arrested in October. The BJP then withdrew its support from the National Front coalition government, triggering its collapse. Elections followed in June 1991. Although the BJP mounted a vigorous campaign strongly flavored with Hindu nationalism, the Congress Party prevailed, thanks to "sympathy votes" cast in memory of Rajiv Gandhi, who had been slain on May 21 by a Tamil suicide bomber while campaigning in southern India.

The BJP's setback at the polls failed to steer the party away from Hindu nationalist agitation. After the 1991 elections, the nationwide campaign for a new Hindu temple in Ayodhya resumed, helped by the presence of a BJP government in the state of Uttar Pradesh. In Delhi, meanwhile, the new Congress Party cabinet under Prime Minister Narasimha Rao deluded itself into thinking that it could manage the BJP by reasoning with its putatively "moderate" elements. Thus did the Congress Party fail to take a firm stand against antisecularist opportunism, even as thousands of VHP and RSS extremists began to descend on Ayodhya in late 1992, egged on by the fiery speeches of BJP politicians. The Uttar Pradesh state government, sympathetic to the radical agenda, deployed insufficient forces to protect the mosque.

On December 6, a large crowd, thick with slogan-shouting, saffron-headbanded RSS and VHP members, brushed aside a thin police cordon and attacked the Babri Masjid, leveling the triple-domed structure with bare hands in just hours as pictures of the frenzied spectacle flashed across the world Rao dismissed the Uttar Pradesh government for failing to maintain law and order and had a number of BJP leaders arrested for inciting violence. But it was too little, too late. Riots exploded across north India. As many as two thousand Muslims and Hindus were killed. Believers in human equality and lovers of justice and peace in every community could only look on in horror as the secularist edifice – meant to forestall such conflict – reeled amid these fearsome intestine broils, where "civil blood [made] civil hands unclean."[32]

After nearly two decades, the Ayodhya problem refuses to go away. A local court tried to depoliticize it by having the Archaeological Survey of India (ASI) study the site in order to learn if an earlier structure exists beneath the razed Babri Masjid, but the ASI's research has so far proved inconclusive, and political controversy dogs the study. The more ardent in the ranks of the Sangh Parivar, meanwhile, still want to build their temple atop the mosque's ruins. In early July 2003, the BJP's executive committee publicly embraced this aim, demonstrating the continued Hindu nationalist belief that rubbing this sore offers electoral advantages.

In the aftermath of the destruction of the mosque, the Union Home Ministry had appointed a retired judge, M. S. Liberhan, to investigate the circumstances that led to the destruction of the mosque. The ministry had instructed the commission to submit its report within a span of three months. In the end, it took the commission sixteen years, 399 meetings, and forty-eight extensions.[33] Within a few months of its submission, an Indian newspaper released its contents. Almost immediately the report came under virulent attack from across the political spectrum. Those hostile to the BJP's antisecular agenda attacked the report on the grounds that it had largely absolved former Prime Minister Narasimha Rao of any responsibility for his failure to forestall the destruction of the mosque.[34] The BJP stoutly rejected the report's view that the destruction of the mosque had been a carefully planned conspiracy.[35] In September 2010, the Allahabed High Court issued a long-awaited but unsatisfying verdict dividing the disputed site among Hindu and Muslim claimants. Appeals of that decision are pending.

[32] William Shakespeare, *Romeo and Juliet*, prologue to act 1, scene 3, line 4.
[33] J. Venkatesan, "Liberhan Commission Submits Report," *The Hindu*, July 1, 2009.
[34] V. Venkatesan, "Indefensible Facts," *Frontline* 26:25 (December 5–18, 2009).
[35] Mridu Khullar, "Report on Mosque Trashing Prompts Fury in India," *Time*, November 24, 2009.

Requiem for a Secular Polity?

Public incitement of sectarian hatred is not the BJP's only weapon in its war on India's secular order. In quieter ways, the party and its Hindu-nationalist affiliates have sought systematically to undermine the principles of equality guaranteed by the Indian constitution. Among the more disturbing of these was the BJP's campaign to rewrite Indian history. Since coming to power nationally in 1998, the party worked to install pro-BJP historians in key academic posts.[36] Under the aegis of the National Council of Educational Research and Training, it worked to change the content of history texts. New schoolbooks extolled the virtues of Hinduism, made dubious claims about the alleged scientific advances of the Vedic Age (ca. 1500 to 500 BCE), and disparaged the advent and role of Islam in South Asia.

Sadly, this is not an altogether new game. To a more limited extent, the Congress Party had used its decades of post-independence political dominance to promote a different ideological slant by looking for scholars with Marxist or at least socialist views to write history books and hold the most important educational positions. Despite its litmus tests, however, the Congress Party managed to appoint scholars with real standing in their fields. The BJP, by contrast, showed no compunction about promoting people whose intellectual credentials are dubious at best.

This is no small matter. As Abraham Lincoln is once supposed to have observed, "The philosophy of the schoolroom in one generation will be the philosophy of government in the next." In a country where the state virtually monopolizes higher education, fundamentally altering the writing of history can affect political attitudes far into the future. The actions of the BJP's ideologues make it clear that they intend just such a reshaping of thought and feeling.

---

[36] Karl Friese, "Hijacking India's History," *New York Times*, December 30, 2002.

Two challenges confront Indian secularism. One is a direct political threat. The BJP and its associated organizations have fostered a significant body of antisecular sentiment and exploited failures and omissions by the Congress Party in order to do so. Worse still, a desperate and rudderless Congress Party – its organizational base tattered, vision occluded, and leadership in disarray – has now drifted into the game of political outbidding. Instead of drawing upon and reinforcing its own salutary tradition of defending principled secularism, Congress has begun to peddle a cleaned-up version of the BJP's Hindu chauvinism.

Apart from the Congress Party, only the two far-left parties, the Communist Party of India and the Communist Party of India (Marxist), have even a notional national presence. But each is burdened by a declining organizational base and a discredited economic ideology. Consequently, apart from idiosyncratic local and regional parties, which may or may not have strong commitments to the secular ideal, the BJP faces no meaningful national challengers. In the absence of a powerful national alternative, will the BJP's Hindu–chauvinist vision inevitably prevail, thereby snuffing out the last embers of Nehruvian secularism? The question does not generate any facile answers.

A second challenge is more intellectual than concretely political, and comes from people who do not share the BJP's brand of virulent antisecularism, but who might be best described as skeptical of secularism in its classic Nehruvian guise and in the market for new or seemingly new alternatives. Some more or less sympathetic observers have started to ring the death knell of the secularist order, often with the observation that secularism is an alien transplant that never had much of a chance at long-term survival within the Indian body politic.[37] Consequently, they assert, it should be allowed

---

[37] Those making this argument include the prominent social psychologist Ashis Nandy and political commentators such as Jug Suraiya. For Nandy's views, see "The Politics of Secularism and the Recovery of

to die a natural death. In its stead, some of its opponents call for an ethic of religious tolerance that they believe can be extracted from India's own organic religious traditions. This argument is flawed and dangerous. India's welter of indigenous spiritual traditions offers no clear teaching in favor of religious tolerance.[38] As with most complex bodies of beliefs, customs, experiences, and discourses, the generalizations that can be drawn are various and may or may not endorse kindness toward "the other." More to the point, this is a plea for feckless voluntarism. Is it not wishful thinking to expect that, in the absence of sanctions against religious hostility, an ethic of religious tolerance will somehow emerge to guide public life?

More to the point, these arguments betray a propensity to draw selectively from India's historical past. Admittedly, some rulers, regardless of faith, displayed an admirable belief in religious pluralism. However, as the political theorist Thomas Pantham has trenchantly argued:

> That there have been such periods or instances of exemplary religious tolerance in India's past is indeed a positive factor or strand in the "effective history" of Indian Society today. But that "effective history" is constituted in a much more important way by the distinctly modern form in which power is exercised in the society. To simplify the matter, it can be said that modernity has transformed the premodern, arbitrary way of exercising power (for instance, by the kings) into codified, disciplined ways of life and thought for the various sections of the society.[39]

Religious Toleration," in *Secularism and Its Critics*, ed. Rajeev Bhargava (New Delhi: Oxford University Press, 1999); Suraiya's position is articulated in "The Death of God: And the Invention of the Human," *Times of India* (Delhi), May 17, 2003.

[38] On this point, see Sanjay Subrahmanyam, "Before the Leviathan: Sectarian Violence and the State in Pre-Colonial India," in *Unraveling the Nation*, ed. Kaushik Basu and Sanjay Subrahmanyam (New Delhi: Penguin Books, 1996).

[39] Pantham, "Indian Secularism and Its Critics," 537.

Those who suggest that religious tolerance can effectually exist apart from secularist institutions may mean well, but theirs is not a serious answer to this crucial question of public policy.

Must the large-scale political and societal pressures that we have been discussing inexorably cause India to abandon its founding commitment to secularism? Are there no countervailing forces that might stem the tide of majoritarian sentiment? Despite the uncertainty that stalks the future of secularism, some clues suggest that all may not yet be lost. It is important to reiterate that the constitutional structure of secularism remains intact. Despite their blatantly antisecular agenda, no BJP stalwarts have suggested any replacement of the constitutional structure of secularism. Also, they remain acutely cognizant of the support that secularism still enjoys in significant quarters of Indian society. For example, significant segments of the Indian press remain deeply committed to secular principles. At another level, large numbers of Indian social scientists, committed to Nehruvian principles of secularism, are standing their ground despite the antisecular tide. Consequently, the BJP and its acolytes publicly insist that they are opposed not to secularism but to "pseudosecularism," one that privileges minority rights at the cost of the majority community.[40]

At another level, the logic of electoral politics has forced the BJP to abandon some of the most dramatic antisecular features of its platform. When it came into office in 1998, the BJP promised to dispense with Article 370 of the Indian constitution. Among other things, this article prohibits the sale of immovable property in the only Muslim-majority state in the Indian union, Jammu and Kashmir, to any non-Kashmiri. Overturning this ban would open the valleys of this

[40] For a discussion of the BJP's attempt to cast itself as a defender of secularism see Upadhyaya, "The Politics of Indian Secularism"; for its critique of pseudosecularism, see Paul R. Brass, "Indian Secularism in Practice," in *Forms of Collective Violence: Riots, Pogroms, and Genocide in Modern India* (New Delhi: Three Essays Collective, 2006).

mountainous state to a flood of Hindu settlers from the plains of north India and beyond, thereby "tipping" the demographics of this contested land. Yet, even after nearly five years in office, the BJP-led coalition government undertook no steps whatsoever to alter the status of Kashmir in the Indian union. Nor did the BJP pursue legislation to bring about a Uniform Civil Code that would finally end the special provisions of Muslim personal law. Thus, even the most ardent elements in the BJP recognize the structural limits on their power. Delving into these nettlesome areas could generate substantial hostility among diverse segments of the Indian polity. Lower-caste voters remain deeply skeptical of the BJP's agenda. In the eyes of many of these Indians, especially in the north, the threat of Brahmin oppression remains all too real. Not surprisingly, lower-caste elected politicians are making common cause with Muslims against the BJP.[41]

The imperatives of electoral politics have also forced the BJP to seek alliances with many regional parties in order to govern at the national level. These parties have often teamed up with the BJP, less because of shared ideology than to gain access to the spoils of office. The devolutionary trend in Indian politics is likely to endure for a long time. Accordingly, any government in New Delhi, BJP-led or otherwise, will have to make electoral adjustments in order to accommodate a plethora of regional parties with diverse political agendas.

From a sociological standpoint, the BJP has already encountered a fundamental and possibly insuperable barrier to the expansion of its electoral base. This may be the gravest impediment to at least the more extreme items on its agenda. The Sangh Parivar has been on a relentless quest to fashion a Hindu monolith.[42] Thankfully, such exertions are unlikely to

[41] Edward Luce, "Faith, Caste, and Poverty," *Financial Times*, July 4, 2003.

[42] It is worth noting that, as a consequence of the innately plural features of Hinduism, some Hindus argue that minorities have little to fear from India being seen as a Hindu country. They fail to recognize that such an argument easily plays into the hands of the kind of virulent religious majoritarianism that the Sangh Parivar represents. I am grateful to

bear much fruit, for Hinduism is inherently plural. It does not have a common sacred text; it lacks a centralized hierarchical, sacerdotal authority; and local – not "all-India" – deities are the focus of everyday devotion. Caste, though formally derecognized under the 1950 constitution, has become a formidable force in Indian politics. For decades now, growing participation by lower-caste voters, particularly in the closely contested districts of north India's thickly settled "Hindi Belt," has been one of the key stories in Indian politics. As a consequence, caste organizations and caste-based parties have proliferated and gathered substantial electoral clout in recent years.[43] Despite its recent resort to more inclusive political rhetoric, the BJP cannot draw in these lower-caste voters without alienating its middle- and upper-caste base.

India's political institutions, though denuded, have demonstrated a remarkable resilience. During the last decade, for example, the Election Commission has roused itself from a long period of somnolence and shown a dramatic capacity to rein in corrupt politicians. Its revival as a political watchdog cannot be overstated. As with any legally constituted body, it has seen routine rotations of senior personnel and considerable variation in the temperament and personality of the top commissioner, a presidential appointee. Yet through all such changes, the commission has displayed great probity and fairness and stood tall in its resolve to uphold the rule of law. In 2002, as the state of Gujarat was about to head to the polls, newly named Chief Election Commissioner James Michael Lyngdoh showed these colors in the case of Gujarat elections. Modi and his backers in New Delhi wanted speeded-up voting in the state, as part of their plan to exploit anti-Muslim sentiment, and did not want to wait for the legally required vetting of the electoral rolls. Although Lyngdoh's principled

Robert L. Hardgrave Jr. of the University of Texas at Austin for underscoring this issue.

[43] For an excellent treatment of this subject see Christophe Jaffrelot, *India's Silent Revolution: The Rise of the Lower Castes* (New York: Columbia University Press, 2003).

stand did not change the election's outcome, he (like several of his recent predecessors) made a valuable contribution just by underscoring the need to respect the integrity of the electoral process.[44] Though the ambit of the Election Commission is limited, it can nevertheless uphold many of the procedural aspects of democracy, thereby protecting the rights of the poor and hitherto disenfranchised minorities. As long as some of these key institutions of democracy remain intact, they may still be able, in conjunction with other social forces, to ward off the seemingly inevitable demise of Indian secularism.

Finally, it's important not to write off the secular elements within India's increasingly vibrant civil society. Economic growth in India has now made possible the steady expansion of a host of civil-society organizations, and many of these have a strong secular orientation. Consequently, they can serve as growing bulwarks against the antisecular forces that threaten the foundations of the Indian polity.[45]

---

[44] V. Venkatesan, "Free, Fair and Secular," *Frontline* 20:17 (August 16–29, 2003).

[45] See the discussion in Rustom Bharucha, *In the Name of the Secular: Contemporary Cultural Activism in India* (Delhi: Oxford University Press, 1998).

6

India's Trajectory – Promises and Challenges

India has attempted a bold experiment in democracy and development. There was no dearth of scholars, public intellectuals, and statesman who had argued that democracy could not take hold in a populous, diverse, and poor country.[1] How could democracy be consolidated in the absence of a substantial middle class?[2] Given the many apparent impediments that were strewn along the pathway toward democracy, the dominant strains of social science literature would lead us to conclude that the prospects for the emergence and consolidation of democracy in India were less than propitious.

Despite these hurdles, democracy did emerge in independent India. In considerable measure the roots of India's democracy must be traced to the genius of the nationalist movement. Its leadership managed to successfully draw on British liberal ideas and instill them in the Indian political context. India's principal nationalist leaders, including Mohandas Gandhi, Jawaharlal Nehru, and the architect of India's constitution, Bhimrao Ambedkar, had shared a pluralistic vision of India.

[1] See, e.g., Selig S. Harrison, *India: The Most Dangerous Decades* (Princeton, NJ: Princeton University Press, 1960).

[2] On socioeconomic prerequisites of democracy, see Seymour M. Lipset, "Some Social and Economic Requisites for Democracy," *American Political Science Review* 53:1 (March 1959): 69–105; Barrington Moore, *Social Origins of Dictatorship and Democracy* (Boston: Beacon Press, 1966), 314–432.

Mohandas Gandhi, the principal exponent of Indian nationalism, converted the elitist Congress Party to a mass-based political organization. The practice of democracy within the Congress Party long before independence laid the foundations for the future consolidation of democracy in India. India's first prime minister, Jawaharlal Nehru, was a liberal who nurtured the practice of democracy and respect for minority rights in postindependent India.[3] The Congress Party under Nehru became an institution that could accommodate a diversity of views and channel the interests of a wide range of actors within the Indian political system for many years. The "Congress system" almost became akin to the Indian political system at this time.[4] Bhimrao Ambedkar, an untouchable who held a doctorate in political science from Columbia University and a law degree from the University of London, chaired the drafting committee of the Indian constitution. The document that he produced has played a critical role over the long haul in expanding political participation through the exercise of universal adult franchise.[5]

This liberal vision of the founding fathers, despite myriad challenges from within, has served India well. India's democratic trajectory, which has witnessed only two years of authoritarian rule (1975–7) and complete civilian control over the military, is a significant achievement in the postcolonial world.[6]

In this section, we will return to the four significant transformations that India has experienced since 1980. First,

[3] Sunil Khilnani, *The Idea of India* (New Delhi: Penguin Books, 1997), 15–60.

[4] Rajni Kothari, "The Congress 'System' in India," *Asian Survey* 4:12 (December 1964): 1161 73.

[5] See Granville Austin, *The Indian Constitution: The Cornerstone of a Nation* (Oxford: Clarendon Press, 1966); Granville Austin, *Working a Democratic Constitution: The Indian Experience* (New Delhi: Oxford University Press, 2001).

[6] Sumit Ganguly, the introduction to *The State of India's Democracy*, ed. Sumit Ganguly, Larry Diamond, and Marc F. Plattner (Baltimore, MD: Johns Hopkins University Press, 2007), ix–xxvii.

democracy and political mobilization gave rise to competitive politics. These phenomena have empowered hitherto marginalized communities but, in turn, have created significant challenges for governance. Second, India's protection of minority rights has been, at best, fitful. Nevertheless, the constitutional dispensation with its commitment to liberal democracy remains largely intact despite severe challenges. Third, economic growth accelerated since 1975 and has gathered considerable momentum since the adoption of more market-friendly policies since the 1991 fiscal crisis. India has subsequently emerged as a substantial player in the world economy. Fourth, and finally, India's foreign policy has abandoned the shibboleths of the Cold War era and taken on a decidedly pragmatic orientation.

However, India's ability to maintain high growth rates and ensure social order depends largely on the ability of the democratic polity to engender substantially higher levels of human development, improve physical infrastructure, and reduce regulatory bottlenecks for productive investment. India will also need to temper the pragmatism of its post–Cold War foreign policy with some regard for normative concerns. This may prove to be a considerable challenge for India's policy makers.[7]

Political Mobilization

Political mobilization represents a success and a continuing challenge for India's democracy. With higher levels of literacy, urbanization, and access to mass communications, the citizenry has become more conscious of its rights.[8] Legislation striving to secure fundamental rights for the poor and the

---

[7] Sumit Ganguly, "India's Machiavellian Turn," *The Wall Street Journal*, July 29, 2010.

[8] Samuel P. Huntington, *Political Order in Changing Societies* (New Haven, CT: Yale University Press, 1968), 1–92.

socially marginalized, such as the right to employment, nutrition, and education, is critical for social progress in a democracy. However, democratic politics can also yield to the politics of populism. We witnessed the rise of both these propensities in Indian politics.[9]

Chapter 4 describes the process by which lower-caste groups and the Hindu nationalist Bharatiya Janata Party (BJP) gathered strength in India. Democratic norms, secularism, and social development suffered when institutions were unable to cope with the rising demands of a greater number of mobilized citizenry. For example, when faced with dramatic new demands and confronted with a court case resulting from certain electoral malfeasances, Indira Gandhi had declared a "state of emergency" between 1975 and 1977. In the process, she had significantly undermined the probity and efficacy of a host of institutions. Worse still, she bypassed state governments and the local state-level Congress Party organizations to reach out directly to the poor through various populist programs in order to gain personal popularity.[10] These efforts did much damage to the democratic norms and procedures that her father had so carefully nurtured and did little to ameliorate the plight of either the rural or urban poor.

More recently, a new set of leaders representing lower-caste groups have resorted to symbolic appeals against discrimination in order to gain personal popularity rather than promote a genuine development agenda. Laloo Prasad Yadav, the chief minister of the state of Bihar, had garnered the

[9] Sumit Ganguly, "Bangladesh and Pakistan," in *Assessing the Quality of Democracy*, ed. Larry Diamond and Leonardo Morlino (Baltimore, MD: Johns Hopkins University Press, 2005), 163–87.

[10] On Indira Gandhi's populism see Steven I. Wilkinson, "Explaining Changing Patterns of Party-Voter Linkages in India," in *Patrons, Clients and Policies: Patterns of Democratic Accountability and Political Competition*, ed. Herbert Kitschelt and Steven I. Wilkinson (New York: Cambridge University Press, 2007), 110–40. For a general account of populism as patronage, see Kanchan Chandra, *Why Ethnic Parties Succeed: Patronage and Ethnic Head Counts in India* (New York: Cambridge University Press, 2004).

support of various lower-caste groups and Muslim voters through populist programs. However, he had done little to generate either economic growth or human development in the state. His party was finally voted out of power in 2005. During this period, Bihar acquired the dubious distinction of becoming one of the poorest states in the country. Another politician with similar propensities is Kumari Mayawati, the chief minister of the large, populous, and poor state of Uttar Pradesh, who heads the Bahujan Samaj Party (BSP). Her proclivity to spend vast sums of money to erect and pro-tect statues of herself, her party's founder Kanshi Ram, and the architect of the Indian constitution and crusader of the rights of the marginalized castes, Bhimrao Ambedkar, is yet another example of the politics of populism at the cost of development. Politics of this order are possible in poor states with large numbers of socially marginalized and illiterate people. Mayawati's calls for self-respect have often served as a substitute for genuine efforts toward promoting economic development and social equity.[11]

Fortunately, all is not lost. The political mobilization of lower-caste groups in the southern state of Tamil Nadu has produced higher levels of human development in comparison to those of Bihar and Uttar Pradesh. The Dravida Munnetra Kazhagam (DMK) and the All India Anna Dravida Munnetra Kazhagam (AIADMK) parties, both expressions of subnationalism, have alternated in power in Tamil Nadu ever since 1967. The rul-ing Congress Party lost elections for the first time in this state during 1967 and has failed to regain power since. Its demise can largely be attributed to its upper-caste orientation in the region. The DMK and the AIADMK substantially increased the representation of lower-caste groups in institutions of edu-cation and employment and attended to human-development tasks like nutrition and literacy with great vigor. Tamil Nadu

---

[11] On Kumari Mayawati, see Sudha Pai, "New Social Engineering Agenda of the Bahujan Samaj Party: Implications for State and National Politics," *South Asia* 32:3 (November 2009): 338–53.

developed one of the most effective institutions governing the public distribution of food in India. The midday meal scheme initiated by the Congress Party government during the 1960s was greatly expanded in 1982.[12] This is the largest school-lunch program in the world, feeding 120 million children, simultaneously engendering child literacy and nutrition – two areas of grave neglect in India. Whereas Tamil Nadu is one of the top eight literate states in India, Uttar Pradesh is among the least literate.[13] Will lower-caste mobilization in the state of Uttar Pradesh lead to the kind of development that Tamil Nadu has witnessed since 1967? The question is far from trivial. Unlike in the 1960s, when India's state-level political institutions were robust, today they are in a state of substantial decay. Consequently, their ability to cope with this rising spate of demands remains in question. Tragically, the states that have the least institutional capacity also face the greatest social demands and economic needs.

Political mobilization in other states, such as Rajasthan and Madhya Pradesh, has generated a new leadership at the grassroots level that has largely replaced the traditional patrons. Perhaps as a consequence, literacy promotion in these two states had been more successful than that in Uttar Pradesh between 1991 and 2001.[14] A more literate socially and economically backward population has produced a generational change in grassroots leadership. It uses information, political contacts, and grassroots connections in order to link political parties to developmental work at the local level. Spurred by such activism of the new leaders, or *naya netas*, Rajasthan and Madhya Pradesh have both done well in the area of literacy promotion

---

[12] On the relationship between lower-caste parties in Tamil Nadu and the evolution of its public distribution system, see A. K. Venkatsubramanian, "The Political Economy of the Public Distribution System in Tamil Nadu," in *Reinventing Public Service Delivery in India*, ed. Vikram K. Chand (Washington, DC, and New Delhi: The World Bank and Sage Publications, 2007), 266–93.

[13] Government of India, *Economic Survey 2008/09* (New Delhi: Oxford University Press, 2009), A122.

[14] Ibid.

and employment generation. Madhya Pradesh has the lowest level of teacher absenteeism in the country – a problem that has posed the greatest challenge to the promotion of literacy in recent times. This has occurred as a result of empowering local governments in the governance of village-level schools. Such social and political processes are likely to engender a positive relationship among political mobilization, growing electoral competition, and development.[15] Even the poverty-stricken state of Bihar voted Yadav's party out of power (2005 and 2010), and it is swiftly transforming itself from a laggard into one of the fastest-growing states in India.

Political mobilization has also led social activists to press for and utilize new legislation in order to address a host of extant failures of governance. To that end the Right to Information Act (RTI), which was passed in 2005, has dramatically expanded their ability to promote greater transparency in governance. For example, nongovernmental organizations like the Mazdoor Kisan Shakti Sangathan (MKSS, or Organization for the Empowerment of Workers and Peasants), which works for literacy promotion and empowerment of the poor people most notably in the state of Rajasthan, played a critical role in the enactment of the RTI. The utilization of this act has had some very salutary consequences for governance. For example, invoking the RTI revealed the corrupt practices of Forest Minister Surupsingh Naik in the state of Maharashtra, and he was successfully prosecuted in 2005.

A nongovernmental organization, Parivartan (or, transformation), effectively deployed the RTI to find substantial leakage in the public-distribution system governing the delivery of subsidized food for the poor in Delhi.[16] Even though the

---

[15] Anirudh Krishna, "Politics in the Middle: Mediating Relationships between the Citizens and the State in Rural North India," in Kitschelt and Wilkinson, *Patrons, Clients and Policies*, 141–58.

[16] Aruna Roy, Nikhil Dey, and Such Pandey, "The Right to Information Act 2005: A Social Development Perspective," in *India: Social Development Report 2008*, ed. Hari M. Mathur (New Delhi: Oxford University Press, 2008), 205–20.

RTI has become a critical tool for empowerment in India, its success will ultimately depend on a more literate citizenry that can fight for its rights.

Pressures from civil society have also resulted in the enactment of the Mahatma Gandhi National Rural Employment Guarantee Act (MGNREGA, 2005), a grand employment-guarantee scheme dedicated largely to the creation of rural public goods. Village-level governments that administer employment-guarantee schemes in rural areas seem to be less corrupt and more accountable than more centralized governance mechanisms.[17] Under the terms of the legislation, unemployed people have a right to compensation even if they cannot find employment in a suitable project. If implemented properly, this act could well be the first effective large-scale welfare program in India.

Higher levels of political mobilization are also reflected in the electoral process. The poor in India are becoming more involved with the electoral process than the rich and are demanding access to the results of economic growth. The 2004 National Election Studies conducted by the Centre for the Study of Developing Societies found that the category of the very poor, peasants, scheduled castes, and scheduled tribes had greater faith in the integrity of the electoral process in India than the average voter. A larger proportion of the poorest 40 percent of the Indian population voted in the 2004 election compared to the wealthiest 20 percent.[18]

The Indian electorate, in turn, has grown from 671 million people in 2004 to 714 million people in 2009. Chapter 3 suggests that a larger and politically mobilized electorate is

---

[17] See, e.g., the classic study by Richard C. Crook and James Manor, "Democracy and Decentralization in Karnataka (India)," in *Democracy in India*, ed. Neeraja G. Jayal (New Delhi: Oxford University Press, 2001), 441–78.

[18] Juan J. Linz, Alfred Stepan, and Yogendra Yadav, "'Nation State' or 'State Nation'? India in Comparative Perspective," in *Democracy and Diversity: India and the American Experience*, ed. K. Shankar Bajpai (New Delhi: Oxford University Press, 2007), 98–101.

demanding greater accountability from the government. The Congress Party–led United Progressive Alliance (UPA) coalition that came to power in 2004 emphasized a strategy of "inclusive growth." The Congress Party and its allies emerged stronger in the 2009 elections after a five-year period, when growth was accompanied with greater emphasis on social justice. The 2009 electoral verdict was the first time in twenty-five years that a party that had completed its full term had came back to power. Although election analysis reveals that this had more to do with the decline of the BJP rather than an increased vote share of the Congress Party, there is evidence to suggest that good governance also made a positive impact on the electoral fortunes of the Congress Party. The ratio of those who were satisfied with the UPA government and wanted to give it another chance, as opposed to those who were not, was 3:1. The positive response to the UPA government's performance has had more to with the assessment of improved household economic conditions than with general economic conditions.[19]

The Congress Party has learned the lesson of the benefits of inclusive growth and swiftly legislated the historic Right to Education Act (2009) within months of coming to power. This act provides for substantially greater resources to primary education than was the case in the past.[20] The right to education and the right to employment have been reinforced with the right to information. Public schooling and employment-generation programs are ridden with corruption. Fortunately, the RTI can be invoked to deal with this endemic problem.

---

[19] Yogendra Yadav and Suhas Palshikar, "Between *Fortuna* and *Virtu*: Explaining the Congress' Ambiguous Victory in 2009," *Economic and Political Weekly* 44:39 (September 26, 2009): 33–46.

[20] Jandhyala B. G. Tilak, "Universalizing Elementary Education: A Review of Progress, Policies and Problems," in *Universalization of Elementary Education in India: Concerns, Conflicts, and Cohesions*, ed. Preet Rustagi (New Delhi: Oxford University Press and Institute of Human Development, 2009), 33–71.

Unfortunately, political mobilization and greater electoral participation among the poor have not yet contributed to the improvement of nutrition levels and public health in India. The distribution of food grains and the expansion of public-health facilities for the poor remains a major challenge in India. India is home to one of the largest numbers of malnourished people in the world. India's infant mortality rate (56) – the number of infants that are unable to survive out of every one thousand live births – was much higher than that of Sri Lanka (5.8) and China (23), and the rate was even a bit higher than that of Bangladesh (54) in 2004.[21] Of children under the age of three years, 45.9 percent were malnourished in 2005 and 2006, a figure not significantly lower than the 47 percent figure that obtained in 1998 and 1999.[22] Corruption in this particular arena is nothing short of rampant. Out of 7.2 billion rupees spent on food subsidy during 2003 and 2004, 4.12 billion rupees worth of food did not reach any family below the poverty line.[23] Will electoral competition put pressure on these areas as it has done for literacy and employment? Or will the politics of populism trump the politics of development, despite the spectacular political and social mobilization witnessed in India? We have no clear-cut answer to these questions.

Political mobilization in India is not always a positive force, however. For example, the recent recrudescence of a Maoist insurgency across significant portions of rural India poses a dramatic challenge to the stability of the Indian state. Recent actions on the part of the Maoists underscore the dangers that lie ahead. In early April 2010, members of a Maoist terrorist organization, the Naxalites, ambushed and killed seventy-six members of India's national Central Reserve Police Force in Dantewada District in the central state of Chattisgarh.

---

[21] C. Sathyamala and N. J. Kurian, "Health Sector: Issues and Challenges," in Mathur, *India: Social Development Report 2008*, 279.

[22] Government of India, *Economic Survey 2008/09*, 262.

[23] S. Mahendra Dev, *Inclusive Growth in India* (New Delhi: Oxford University Press, 2008), 117.

This was the Naxalites' most brazen and successful attack on India's internal security forces since their resurgence sometime in 2004. According to some estimates, sixteen out of India's twenty-eight states now face some level of Naxalite activity, leading Prime Minister Manmohan Singh to characterize them as the single most important security threat facing the country.[24]

The origins of the movement can be traced to 1967 to a region known as Naxalbari in the eastern state of West Bengal. At that time, it was mostly a peasant-based rebellion that drew its inspiration from Mao Tse-Tung's ideas of agrarian unrest. It peaked in the late 1960s and spread to West Bengal's capital, Calcutta. However, the state government managed to brutally suppress the movement especially as it metamorphosed into an extortion racket with an ideological patina.[25]

A number of explanations abound for the recrudescence of the Naxalites movement nearly three decades since their initial suppression. Some commentators have attributed it to India's embrace of economic liberalization and growing income inequalities; some attribute it to poor governance and have sought to link it to the opening up of tribal lands for mineral extraction and industrialization.[26] None of these explanations can be deemed complete. However, there is little question of the Maoist mobilization of extant grievances in India's more remote areas, which have not benefited much from the country's surge of economic growth. Consequently, the Indian state will have to fashion a strategy that combines coercion with improved governance in order to tackle this menace.

[24] Andrew Buncombe, "The Big Question: Who Are the Naxalites and Will They Topple the Indian Government?" *The Independent*, April 8, 2010.

[25] Ranjit Kumar Gupta, *The Crimson Agenda: Maoist Protest and Terror* (New Delhi: Wordsmiths, 2004).

[26] See, e.g., Prakash Singh, *The Naxalite Movement in India* (New Delhi: Rupa, 2006); also see Sudeep Chakravarti, *Red Sun: Travels in Naxalite Country* (New Delhi: Penguin Books, 2008).

Institutional Pillars

During the past three decades, the Indian Supreme Court has played an active role in improving governance and in securing the basic rights of the Indian citizens, despite concerns about the court's becoming a suprademocratic authority.[27] The Supreme Court emerged from an era of subservience to the executive between 1977 and 1979, and actively encouraged a new form of jurisprudence: public-interest litigation. Two noted members of the Supreme Court, Justice P. N. Bhagwati and Justice V. R. Krishna Iyer were instrumental in bringing about this important judicial innovation.

Such litigation has significantly benefited the country's ordinary citizens. A number of examples of the beneficial effects of the court's activism can be cited. First, the court linked the right to education to the right to a livelihood in 1993, which set a precedent for treating education as a fundamental right more than a decade and half before the Right to Education Act (2009) was passed.[28] Second, the right to food was linked to the right to a livelihood in a landmark judgment (2002). This opinion of the court led to the distribution of food in Rajasthan and helped avert starvation deaths.[29] Third, the court directed the buses of the government-owned Delhi Transport Corporation to use environmentally friendly compressed natural gas rather than diesel as a fuel (2002) – a

[27] On a variety of views on judicial activism, see Upendra Baxi, "The Avatars of Indian Activism: Explorations in the Geographies of [In]justices," in *Fifty Years of the Supreme Court of India*, ed. S. K. Verma (New Delhi: Oxford University Press, 2000), 150–209; Pratap B. Mehta, "The Rise of Judicial Sovereignty," *Journal of Democracy* 18:2 (April 2007): 70–83; Rajeev Dhawan, "Governance by Judiciary: Into the Next Millennium," in *Indian Judiciary and Politics: The Changing Landscape*, ed. B. D. Dua and Rekha Saxena (New Delhi: Manohar, 2007); also see B. N. Kirpal, Ashok H. Desai, Gopal Subramaniam, Rajeev Dhavan, and Raju Ramachandran, eds., *Supreme but Not Infallible: Essays in Honour of the Supreme Court of India* (New Delhi: Oxford University Press, 2000).

[28] Tilak, "Universalizing Elementary Education," 33–4.

[29] Reetika Khera, "Right to Food Act: Beyond Cheap Promises," *Economic and Political Weekly* 44:29 (July 18, 2009): 40–4.

move that the national government unsuccessfully opposed.[30] This opinion of the court has had a dramatic impact in reducing Delhi's air pollution. Thanks to the court's decision, the Delhi Transport Corporation runs the world's largest fleet of eco-friendly buses.

Other institutions have also shown signs of renewal. For example, we have previously described the renewed role of the Election Commission as a guardian of Indian democracy. We want to reiterate that this institution is pivotal for the future of India's democracy. Chief Election Commissioner T. N. Seshan (1990–6) played a significant role in revitalizing the commission's powers and fashioning a model code of conduct for election campaigns. Under his watch, national government employees, were drafted for election-monitoring duties instead of state government employees, whom state-level political parties and functionaries could easily influence. Additionally, voter identity cards were introduced despite opposition from much of the political class. Finally, the commission has introduced electronic voting machines thereby reducing the possibilities of electoral fraud.

Nevertheless, the governance of election funding remains a significant challenge in India. India does not have substantial public funding for elections, nor is it possible to place significant limits on electoral spending. Even though a candidate's spending has to be within permissible and reasonable limits, the Representation of the People Amendment Act (1975) removed all expenditure limits on political parties. Limited progress in disciplining election spending has been made by reducing the campaign period to fourteen days. Audited company donations are now 100 percent tax deductible. All donations of amounts greater than $450 need to be reported. Despite these measures, unaudited election funds abound.[31]

[30] Subhendu Rajan Raj, "Supreme Court Environmental Crusade," in Dua and Saxena, *Indian Judiciary and Politics*, 221–38.

[31] On election funding, see Easwaran Sridharan, "Electoral Finance Reform: The Relevance of International Experience," in Chand, *Reinventing Public Service Delivery in India*, 362–88.

Secularism

The constitutional commitment to rights in India also manifests itself in the realm of religion. India is a multiethnic and multireligious society that formally accords equal respect to all faiths. We have described the reasons that have led to dramatic departures from this commitment in four important cases – when the Sikh preacher Bhindranwale was courted by the Congress Party in the 1980s in order to undermine the Akali Dal, a regional political party in Punjab; when a Muslim woman was not allowed alimony after her divorce as a result of the pressures from the conservative Muslim community (1985) and for fear of an electoral backlash; when the Babri mosque was allowed to be demolished to appease Hindu nationalist sentiments (1992); and when thousands of Muslims were mercilessly killed in Godhra (Gujarat, 2002) after some Muslims had set fire to a train compartment that led to the death of more than fifty Hindus.

The practice of secularism, however imperfect, has survived. Electoral power has provided Muslims in India an important tool to punish political parties that seek to restrict their rights. For example, in the 2004 elections, Muslims voted as a bloc against the BJP, even though the party was able to court some high-profile leaders of the Muslim community, such as the Imam of Jama Masjid in New Delhi. Minority rights have fared much better under the UPA government. That said, it should be underscored that many within the UPA are willing to uphold secular principles on the basis of electoral exigencies rather than fundamental ethical and moral convictions. Consequently, the political adherence to secular practices in India may now lack a more intrinsic basis.

The Economic Transformation

The social transformation that we described earlier has also been accompanied by an economic transformation. An economy that grew at an average annual rate of 3.4 percent between 1956 and 1975 is now one of the fastest-growing major economies in the world in the new millennium.[32] We contend that the Indian case is an important outlier. Much of the literature on political economy suggests that the presence of hard or authoritarian states that could discipline capital and push them in the direction of export-led industrialization explains rapid economic growth in Asia. India's economic growth in a democracy, in which the increasingly mobilized citizenry mattered, throws light on a different kind of political and economic pathway to economic growth. This transition resembles cases of crisis-driven economic change in the Western world, such as the shift to Keynesianism in the United States after the Great Depression or the one that led to the adoption of neoliberal economic policies in the 1980s.[33]

How did this transition occur? First, we describe the changes in technocratic convictions among policy makers regarding the benefits of a more market-friendly approach to economic development. India's economic bureaucracy and the civil service had conducted substantial research on the reasons that produced low levels of productivity and competitiveness in India. This research within the government from the mid-1970s had created a critical mass of technocrats who were impatient for change in 1991. Some changes occurred

[32] The figures are from the World Development Indicators, The World Bank, accessed through the National University of Singapore's library Web site.

[33] On economic transitions in the West, see Albert O. Hirschman, "How the Keynesian Revolution Was Exported to the United States, and Other Comments," in *The Political Power of Economic Ideas*, ed. Peter A Hall (New York: Cambridge University Press, 1989), 347–60; Peter A. Hall, "Policy Paradigms, Social Learning and the State," *Comparative Politics* 25:3 (1993): 275–96. On the Indian transition and its relationship with these transitions, see Rahul Mukherji, "Interests, Wireless Technology, and Institutional Change: From Government Monopoly to Regulated Competition in Indian Telecommunications," *Journal of Asian Studies* 68:2 (May 2009): 491–518.

during the 1980s, but political exigencies thwarted substantial industrial deregulation and export promotion.

Second, the balance-of-payments crisis in 1991, when India was two weeks away from defaulting on its foreign-exchange commitments, led to the dramatic changes in trade and industrial policies. The severity of the crisis was such that opposition to a new set of economic incentives from Indian industry, which was accustomed to a regime of stringent industrial controls and high levels of trade protection, did not materialize. India's autarkic industrialization was heavily dependent on imports, and access to these imports would depend on International Monetary Fund (IMF) funding during a crisis. Some sections of Indian industry in the more competitive sectors, such as engineering, software, and services, were also genuinely in favor of policy changes needed for promoting competitiveness. The political class was also not immune to the severity of the crisis. This environment produced a window of opportunity for reformers within the technocracy to push the economy irreversibly in the direction of trade, industrial, and financial reforms that became the basis of the high-growth trajectory.

The 1991 economic reforms, and the gradual but significant reforms thereafter, have produced a substantial economic transformation. A number of indicators of India's success can be adduced. The success of the highly export-oriented IT and service sector worth $71 billion has earned India the title of the "back office of the world."[34] India has more than 780 million mobile telephone connections (December 2010) and is adding more than eight million new connections every month, in what is considered to be one of the fastest-growing and most efficient telecommunications sectors in

---

[34] For the size of the information technology and services sector in India see the Web site of the National Association of Software and Service Companies, http://www.nasscom.in. For the latest figures for the number of telephone lines in India and monthly growth rates, see the Web site of the Telecom Regulatory Authority of India, http://www.trai.gov.in (accessed December 29, 2010).

the world. India's stock-market reforms have helped its companies to raise substantial funds in its booming stock exchanges. India's banks, financial organizations, and the private civil-aviation sector have become competitive.[35] Inward foreign direct investment, which was $24 billion during the period between 1992 and 2002, was $25.5 billion between January and November 2009.[36] A country that had banished foreign investors from its territory by reducing the maximum permissible foreign equity in Indian firms to a low level of 40 percent in 1974 became a major foreign investor after 2003. In 2007, Indian companies had invested $12.8 billion in buying foreign companies, thus making India the second-most important foreign investor among the emerging economies.[37] Indian manufacturing exports were also competitive in areas such as gems and jewelry, automobile parts, and pharmaceuticals.

Yet significant challenges to the growth process abound. The condition of Indian ports does not augur well for its foreign trade. They carry 95 percent of India's trade by volume and 70 percent by value. Ports should have been easy to reform because they are highly amenable to private-sector orientation and serve consumers who are driven by considerations of competition and efficiency. Unfortunately, the

---

[35] For financial-sector reforms, see Arvind Panagariya, *India: The Emerging Giant* (New Delhi and New York: Oxford University Press, 2008), 214–58; John Echeverri-Gent, "Politics of Market Micro-Structure: Towards a New Political Economy of India's Equity Market Reform," in *India's Economic Transition: The Politics of Reform*, ed. Rahul Mukherji (New Delhi: Oxford University Press, 2007), 328–58.

[36] See the Web site of the Department of Industrial Policy and Promotion, Ministry of Commerce and Industry – Government of India for the latest information, http://dipp.nic.in/fdi_statistics/india_FDI_November2009.pdf (accessed December 29, 2010).

[37] India was just behind China, which had invested $16.1 billion during the same year. The Indian figure was more substantial if you considered the fact that the Chinese economy is 2.5 times the size of the Indian economy. See Nagesh Kumar, "Internationalization of Indian Enterprises: Patterns, Strategies, Ownership Advantages, and Implications," *Asian Economic Policy Review* 3:2 (December 2008): 242–65.

current bidding and tariff-making procedures do not favor considerations of efficiency and profitability. The Department of Shipping runs the port trusts, and the government has successfully opposed its corporatization. The result is that large ships often dock in the nearby ports of Colombo, Singapore, and Dubai, and smaller vessels are used to deliver goods to the Indian ports. Indian ports demand more time and money to clear goods than ports in the neighboring countries and thereby serve as an important bottleneck to enhanced external trade.[38]

Rent seeking afflicted even the booming telecommunications sector while the government was awarding the 2G spectrum during 2008. The Department of Telecommunications (DOT) disregarded the recommendations of the regulator and the written suggestions made by the Prime Minister's Office, the Ministry of Finance, and the Ministry of Law and Justice. It made unilateral decisions about bids for the spectrum. A formal report of the comptroller and auditor general of India found that there was a significant loss of revenue for the exchequer and that merit had been compromised. The DOT adopted an indefensible policy of first-come, first-served, but then arbitrarily decided to issue letters of intent to only those parties who had applied for a license between March 2006 and September 25, 2007. After taking a much longer time to process the applications than the prescribed period, the DOT gave successful applicants less than an hour to collect their letters of intent, informing them by a press release. The successful bidders were given less than half a day to comply with the terms and conditions in the letters of intent. Obviously, those who had been tipped in advance stood to gain.[39]

[38] Rahul Mukherji, "Regulation and Infrastructure Development in India: Telecommunications, Power and Ports," in *Public Service Delivery in India*, ed. Vikram Chand (New Delhi: Oxford University Press, 2010): 184–93.

[39] Report of the Comptroller and Auditor General of India, *Performance Audit Report on the Issue of Licenses and Allocation of 2G Spectrum by the Department of Telecommunications, Ministry of Communications and*

This episode created much consternation within Parliament during December 2010 and January 2011. The opposition refused to allow Parliament to carry on its business. The prime minister, whose personal integrity is beyond question, was accused by the opposition of having turned a blind eye to spectacular corruption.[40] The promotion of competition in the absence of transparent regulation can harm the one sector in which India's growth surpasses China's growth. This saga demonstrates the need for strengthening independent and accountable regulatory institutions.

Areas characterized by "mass politics," where a large number of workers are well organized, have been even more difficult to reform than the ports sector.[41] For example, India's power sector remains unprofitable, and private companies are unable to play a substantial role in a market in which farmers refuse to pay electricity bills. Rich farmers, who are less numerous but more organized as a pressure group than marginal farmers, are able to exert considerable electoral influence on the government. The provision of free electricity for farmers is a major contributor to India's growing fiscal deficit.[42]

Second, India's labor laws protect less than 10 percent of India's 455 million workers who suffer from low wages and no job security. These labor laws impede the productivity

Information Technology (New Delhi: Union Government, 2010), iii–viii, 12–24, 28–30.

[40] Swaminathan A. Aiyar, "How to Prevent Licensing Scams," The Economic Times (New Delhi), December 12, 2010. See also, http://economictimes. indiatimes.com/opinion/columnists/swaminathan-s-a-aiyar/How-to-prevent-licensing-scams/articleshow/7085734.cms (accessed January 6, 2011).

[41] See Ashutosh Varshney, "Mass Politics or Elite Politics? Understanding the Politics of India's Economic Reforms," in Mukherji, India's Economic Transition: The Politics of Reforms, 158–64; Ashutosh Varshney, "India's Democratic Challenge," Foreign Affairs 86:2 (March/April 2007): 93–106.

[42] Rahul Mukherji, "Managing Competition: Politics and the Building of Independent Regulatory Institutions," in Mukherji, India's Economic Transition, 312–27.

of Indian companies and keep the vast majority of Indian workers out of the fold of any form of legal protection. Unreasonable labor laws discourage investment and affect productivity.They encourage small-scale and capital-intensive production activities, which obstruct the realization of comparative advantage in manufacturing in a labor-abundant economy.[43] The few and better organized workers in the trade unions are able to realize their benefits at the cost of the bulk of the working population. Encompassing trade unions have produced robust welfare in the advanced industrial world. Inclusive growth in India demands that more jobs are shifted from the agricultural to the manufacturing sector. Moreover, India has a larger young population compared to that of China.This can only become an asset if more numerous and steady employment opportunities are generated in the Indian manufacturing industry. This calls for substantial changes in India's labor laws.

Third, numerous regulations and clearances remain despite the fact that industrial licensing, or the need to seek permission before initiating commercial activity, was largely abolished in the path-breaking Industrial Policy of 1991. Investors still need governmental clearances in areas such as labor, land, pollution, water supply, power, taxation, and transport links from the state and Central governments. These clearances from the political class in the Central government and at the state levels are still ridden with rent-seeking and political considerations that obstruct investments.

Fourth, land acquisition is a major impediment in places where the government or the investor is unable to win the consent of the population. If the local population proves unwilling, acquiring land for commercial purposes becomes politically untenable. A need exists to gravitate toward a regulatory framework that marries the needs of the population who are unwilling to move from their existing sources of

[43] Suresh D. Tendulkar and T. A. Bhavani, *Understanding India: Post-1991 India* (New Delhi: Oxford University Press, 2007), 138–48.

livelihood with the positive role that investments can play in addressing some of those concerns.[44]

The Transformation of Foreign Policy

Since the 1980s, India's foreign policy has steadily, if fitfully, shed much of the ideological baggage that had freighted its conduct. Little reason exists to believe that the country's foreign policy will revert to its previously normative and ideational orientation. As discussed in Chapter 5, the end of the Cold War had a dramatic impact on the key assumptions that had long guided India's foreign policy. Faced with the Soviet collapse and the concomitant end of the Indo–Soviet security nexus, India's policy makers were compelled to chart a new course. The new orientation displayed a remarkable pragmatism and sought to ensure that India would not be marginalized in the emergent global order. To that end its policy makers improved relations with the United States, made friendly overtures toward the People's Republic of China and pursued a policy of engagement with the hitherto neglected states of Southeast Asia. India also dispensed with its residual reservations about the significance and the utility of the use of force in international politics. To that end, its policy makers chose to test nuclear weapons overtly despite the full knowledge that such a decision would almost inevitably result in large-scale multilateral sanctions.

Since these dramatic shifts in the orientation of India's foreign policy, with the exception of the leftist political parties, a broad consensus has emerged across the Indian political spectrum about the direction of the country's foreign policy.

[44] Naushad Forbes, "Doing Business in India: What Has Liberalization Changed?" in *Economic Policy Reforms and the Indian Economy*, ed. Annie O. Krueger (New Delhi: Oxford University Press, 2002), 129–68; Rahul Mukherji, "Special Economic Zones in India: Recent Developments and Future Prospects," Working Paper 30 (Singapore: Institute of South Asian Studies, 2008): 1–15.

Most political parties share the view that India should, to the extent possible, seek a multipolar global order and one that enhances India's strategic autonomy. They also do not envisage any abandonment of India's nuclear arsenal. The successful conclusion of the 2008 U.S.-India nuclear agreement tacitly cemented the country's status as a nuclear-weapons state.

Despite the dexterity that its policy makers have displayed during the last three decades, India's foreign policy still confronts serious, if not daunting, challenges in the years ahead. Apart from dealing with China's seemingly inexorable rise, India will still have to successfully manage the nascent relationship with the United States and maintain a small but robust and secure nuclear-weapons arsenal. It will also have to devise the means to strengthen its foreign-policy–making apparatus to cope with these important tasks effectively. How India manages these key issues will determine the success of its foreign policy in the foreseeable future.

Index